Nineteenth-Century Britain: A Very Short Introduction

Very Short Introductions available now:

Christopher Harvie and H. C. G. Matthew

NINETEENTH-CENTURY BRITAIN

A Very Short Introduction

OXFORD
UNIVERSITY PRESS

OXFORD
UNIVERSITY PRESS

Great Clarendon Street, Oxford OX2 6DP

Oxford University Press is a department of the University of Oxford.
It furthers the University's objective of excellence in research, scholarship,
and education by publishing worldwide in

Oxford New York

Auckland Bangkok Buenos Aires Cape Town Chennai
Dar es Salaam Delhi Hong Kong Istanbul Karachi Kolkata
Kuala Lumpur Madrid Melbourne Mexico City Mumbai Nairobi
São Paulo Shanghai Taipei Tokyo Toronto

Oxford is a registered trade mark of Oxford University Press
in the UK and in certain other countries

Published in the United States
by Oxford University Press Inc., New York

Text © Christopher Harvie and the estate of H. C. G. Matthew 2000

The moral rights of the authors have been asserted

Database right Oxford University Press (maker)

Text first published in *The Oxford Illustrated History of Britain* 1984
First published as a Very Short Introduction 2000

British Library Cataloguing in Publication Data

Data available

Library of Congress Cataloging in Publication Data

Data available

ISBN 978 0-19-285398-1

19 20 18

Typeset by RefineCatch Ltd, Bungay, Suffolk
Printed in Great Britain by
Ashford Colour Press Ltd, Gosport, Hants.

Contents

List of Illustrations

The publisher and the author apologize for any errors or omissions in the above list. If contacted they will be pleased to rectify these at the earliest opportunity.

List of Maps

Chapter 1
Reflections on the Revolutions

In 1881 the young Oxford historian Arnold Toynbee delivered his *Lectures on the Industrial Revolution*, and in so doing made it as distinct a 'period' of British history as the Wars of the Roses. This makes it easy, but misleading, to conceive of an age of the 'dual revolution' – political in France and industrial in Britain. But while the storming of the Bastille was obvious *fact*, industrialization was gradual and relative in its impact. It showed up only in retrospect, and notions of 'revolution' made less sense to the British, who shuddered at the word, than to the Europeans, who knew revolution at close quarters. A Frenchman was in fact the first to use the metaphor – the economist Adolphe Blanqui in 1827 – and Karl Marx gave the concept general European currency after 1848.

This makes the historian's task awkward, balancing what is significant now against what was significant then. The first directs us to industrial changes, new processes developing in obscure workshops; the second reminds us how slowly the power of the pre-industrial elites ebbed, how tenacious religion proved in the scientific age. Only around 1830 were people conscious of substantial and permanent industrial change; it took another 20 years to convince even the middle class that it had all been for the better.

Statistics and Context

Should there not be a simple factual record of developments? In theory, yes. But the age of the 'supremacy of fact' was so ever-changing and obsessively individualistic that recording and assessing facts was another matter. There was no official population Census until 1801; before then there had been real controversy about whether the population of Britain was growing or shrinking. Although the Census subsequently developed into a sophisticated implement of social analysis, covering occupations and housing conditions, this was as gradual a process as the systematic mapping of the country, carried out by the Ordnance Survey in stages between 1791 and the 1860s. The ideology of *laissez-faire* and actual government retrenchment adversely affected statistical compilation, as fewer goods or businesses were regulated or taxed. (Continental autocracies were, by comparison, enthusiastic collectors of data about their little industrial enterprises.) So controversy still rages over some elementary questions – notably about whether industrialization did the mass of the people any good.

At this point, modern politics casts its shadow. Toynbee's contemporaries agreed with Karl Marx that capitalist industrialization had, by 1848, failed to improve the condition of the working class. After 1917 Soviet Russia seemed to demonstrate a viable alternative: 'planned industrialization'. But the costs of this, in human life and liberty, soon became apparent and, with the 'developing world' in mind, liberal economists restated the case for industrialization achieved through the operation of the free market. Even in the short term, they argued, and faced with the problem of providing resources for investment, British capitalism had increased both investment and living standards. The results of this vehement dispute have been inconclusive. They have also been restricted in their geographical context, considering that British economic development had direct, and far from fortunate, effects on Ireland, India, and the Southern States of the USA.

Consciousness

If there are problems with statistics and context, there is also the question of consciousness. Industrialization as a concept was only germinating in the 1820s. Whatever the governing elite thought about economic doctrines, as magistrates and landowners their watchword was stability, their values were still pre-industrial. But by 1829 the trend to industrialization became, quite suddenly, unmistakable. Only 11 years after the last of Jane Austen's novels a raucous new voice pictured the 'Signs of the Times' in the *Edinburgh Review*: 'We remove mountains, and make seas our smooth highway; nothing can resist us. We war with rude nature; and by our resistless engines, come off always victorious, and loaded with spoils.' Thomas Carlyle summed up, vividly and emotionally, a plethora of contemporary impressions: the change from heroic to economic politics that Sir Walter Scott had described in the Waverley novels, the planned factory community of Robert Owen's New Lanark, the visionary politics of desperate handloom weavers, the alarm and astonishment shown by European visitors. Only a few months later, his word was made iron in George Stephenson's *Rocket*.

But can we gain from such images a consistent set of concepts which are relevant both to us and to the age itself? G. M. Young, its pioneer explorer, in *The Portrait of an Age* (1936), saw his actors 'controlled, and animated, by the imponderable pressure of the Evangelical discipline and the almost universal faith in progress'. But Young's history – 'the conversation of the people who counted' – was pretty elitist history, which neglected the mass of the people – miners and factory hands, Irish cotters, and London street arabs – or identified them solely as 'problems'. The perception, at its most acute in Leo Tolstoy's *War and Peace*, that great movements stem from millions of individual decisions reached by ordinary people, was lacking. Few of the British contemporaries of his French and Russian soldiers shared the views of 'the people who counted': as far as we know, only a minority of them

1. 'A voluptuary under the horrors of digestion'. George IV, as prince of Wales in 1792, surrounded by evidence of his extravagances – unpaid gambling debts (despite £161,000 voted by Parliament in 1787 to bail him out) and visible through the window his opulent London residence of Carlton House. A cartoon of a favourite victim by James Gillray, 1757–1815, the most brilliant and merciless of British caricaturists

saw the inside of a church, and from what they wrote and read they had little enough faith in progress. Yet, however constrained their freedom of action, the decisions of those subjected to the 'monstrous condescension of posterity' are crucial. We have to attend to them.

The Rule of Law

E. P. Thompson, who coined the phrase above, has argued that a continuing frame of interpretation did exist: the law. No matter how partial its administration – and in the eighteenth century this was often brutally apparent – 'the rule of law' was still regarded as a common possession. This claim remained valid after the industrial impact. In 1832, as a young MP, Thomas Babington Macaulay argued in favour of political reform to protect the rule of law from the exercise of arbitrary power: 'People crushed by law have no hopes but from power. If laws are their enemies, they will be enemies to law.' Let the law 'incorporate' new groups, and these would defer to the state system. This philosophy balanced the 'revolutionary' consequences of industrial changes, and the frequent attempts to create from these a new politics.

The evolution of law, moreover, provided a model for other social and political changes. 'The most beautiful and wonderful of the natural laws of God', in an Oxford inaugural lecture of 1859, turned out to be economics, but they might as well have been jurisprudence or geology. Personal morality, technical innovation, the very idea of Britain: the equation of law with progress bore all these together on its strong current.

Among all classes, the old morality – bribery and unbelief, drinking, wenching, and gambling – gradually became regarded as archaic if not antisocial. As well as 'vital religion', rationalist enlightenment, retailed from Scotland or France, and cheaper consumer goods indicated that life could be longer and more refined. Where Samuel Pepys had regarded his Admiralty subordinates' wives as legitimate fringe

5

2. A family group by John Harden of Brathay Hall, 1826. Harden, 1772–1847, was a talented amateur artist who lived in modest comfort in the Lake District, then a notable centre of English intellectual life: William Wordsworth, Thomas de Quincey, and Thomas Arnold of Rugby were neighbours. Harden's paintings convey a perceptive impression of 'English Biedermeier' middle-class life

benefits, James Boswell, equally amorous, agonized about his wife and family, foreshadowing new moral imperatives – whether engendered by the evils of corruption or slavery, proletarian unrest, the French, or the wrath of the God so dramatically depicted by William Blake.

The onus of proof was on the status quo. Did it elevate? Did it improve? The English traveller who, in 1839, was appalled to find that the Hungarians had no sailing boats on their waterways, when their Muslim neighbours had *dhows* on the Danube, was typical in regarding this, whatever the reasons for it – the interests of oarsmen and horsemen, the free transport entitlement of Hungarian nobles, sheer loathing of everything Turkish – as a case of 'sinister interests' blocking reform and progress.

'Progress'

Neither 'progress' nor the rule of law were inevitable but had to be fought for, against internal and external enemies: 'old corruption' and new disaffection at home, powerful rivals abroad. Progress meant moral development, not economic or political manipulation – the values expressed, say, by the hero of Mrs Craik's *John Halifax, Gentleman* (1857):

> Nothing that could be done did he lay aside until it was done; his business affairs were kept in perfect order, each day's work being completed with the day. And in the thousand-and-one little things that were constantly arising, from his position as magistrate and landowner, and his general interest in the movements of the time, the same system was invariably pursued. In his relations with the world outside, as in his own little valley, he seemed determined to 'work while it was day.' If he could possibly avoid it, no application was ever unattended to; no duty left unfinished; no good unacknowledged; no evil unremedied, or at least unforgiven.

The rule of law was an English tradition, but its role as an ideology of 'efficient' government had in part been created on Britain's internal frontiers. Dragging their country out of its backwardness, the Scots had used their distinctive legal institutions as instruments for consolidating landed capital, for exploring and ordering 'civil society'. In Edinburgh, Adam Smith, William Robertson, Adam Ferguson, and David Hume wove economics, history, sociology, and philosophy together with jurisprudence to produce the complex achievement of the Scots Enlightenment. Figures such as Patrick Colquhoun, James Mill, and the 'Edinburgh Reviewers' transmitted its values south. Ireland's contribution was quite different. 'The law', Dean Swift had written, 'presumes no Catholic to breathe in Ireland.' Protestant law had, by definition, to be coercive. Not surprisingly, Ireland saw the creation of Britain's first state-organized police force, in 1814.

Although legal campaigns helped to end the serfdom of Scots colliers and salt-workers in 1799, and the British Empire's slave trade in 1807, Scots and English cottars benefited little from their role in the 'improvement' of their countryside. Law was more than ever the tool of property: a function which unified the local elites of a still-disparate society when assault from Europe threatened. The clan chiefs and lairds who had rallied to the French-backed Charles Edward in 1745 were now landowners who had no common cause with revolutionaries. Jacobinism was as alien to them as Jacobitism. But the ensuing use of law to enforce national solidarity and safeguard economic changes was to face it with its most formidable test.

Chapter 2
Industrial Development

A greybeard in 1815, who could remember the panic in London as the Jacobites marched through Manchester in 1745, would have been struck by one important international change – the reversal in the positions of Britain and France. This was not simply the result of over 20 years of war culminating in victory at Waterloo, but of consistent industrial development and the take-over of important markets. British blockades destroyed the economy of the great French seaports: grass grew in the streets of Bordeaux, and meanwhile Britain annexed something like 20 per cent of world trade, and probably about half the trade in manufactured goods.

Britain and France

Industrial development did not follow a predetermined, predictable route to success. The process was gradual and casual. Adam Smith regarded industry with suspicion; even in the 1820s, economists doubted whether technology could improve general living standards. Britain had certainly advanced in the century which followed Gregory King's estimate, in 1688, that mining, manufacturing, and building produced a fifth of the gross national income of England and Wales. (The *British* figure would be less, as it included backward Scotland and Ireland.) By 1800, estimates put the British 'manufacturing' figure at 25 per cent of national income, and trade and transport at 23 per cent. This sort of growth, however, was not beyond French capabilities. What marked Britain off were qualitative changes, notably in patterns of marketing, technology, and government intervention – and, at 33 per cent of national product in 1800, capitalist agriculture. While revolution retarded French farming by enhancing peasant rights, in Britain feudal title became effective ownership, the key to commercial exploitation.

In 1745 France's population, at 21 million, was double that of Britain. The French economy, thanks to royal patronage and state control, not only had a huge output but was technologically inventive and grew as rapidly as Britain's. But technology in Britain was developed by new requirements, while in France it was checked not only by government interference but by the bounty of traditional resources. France still produced ample wood for charcoal; British ironmasters had to turn to coal. France had a huge woollen industry integrated with peasant farming; in Britain, enclosure and growing agricultural efficiency set limits to such domestic industries, and encouraged the building of large industrial plants which needed water or steam power or systematized production. Above all, Britain had already won the trade war by the 1770s, pushing France out of the Spanish territories, out of India and Canada – with even the loss of the American colonies soon made good by the rise of the cotton trade.

Population

In 1801, the first official Census found that England had 8.3 million people, Scotland 1.63 million, Wales 587,000, and Ireland 5.22 million. This settled the debate on population: it seemed to have risen by about 25 per cent since 1750, a rate of increase 50 per cent greater than the European norm. Debate still continues about why. The death-rate fell some time before 1750 (as a result of improved food supplies and better hygiene, and a diminution in the killing power of epidemics) and this was then reflected in a rising birth-rate as the greater number of surviving children reached breeding age.

In Britain, increased manufacturing activity, and the vanishing of the family farm, made children a valuable source of income. 'Away, my boys, get children,' advised the agricultural writer Arthur Young, 'they are worth more than they ever were.' In Ireland, population growth surfed along on a different wave: the landlords who wanted higher rents, and the cultivation of potatoes from the 1720s on. The latter increased the nutritive output of a patch of land by a factor of three; the former realized that a rising population on additional farms meant that each acre might yield three times its rent. The population consequently doubled in the 50 years between 1780 and 1831:

	Population (in millions)			
	1780 (est.)	1801	1831	1851
England	7.1	8.30	13.1	16.92
Wales	0.43	0.59	0.91	1.06
Scotland	1.4	1.63	2.37	2.90
Ireland	4.05	5.22	7.77	6.51
Total UK	12.98	15.74	24.15	27.39
England (as %)	54.7%	52.7%	54.2%	61.8%

A recent calculation has suggested that in the early nineteenth century British agriculture was 2.5 times more productive than that of France, itself much more efficient than that of the rest of Europe. The result was that a population on the move from country to town, and at the same time increasing, could be fed. In 1801 about 30 per cent of the mainland British lived in towns, and 21 per cent in towns of over 10,000 population – a far higher percentage than in any north European country. Industrial towns, however, accounted for less than a quarter of this figure. Their inhabitants were outnumbered by the numbers living in seaports, dockyard towns, and regional centres. London, already a metropolis without parallel, had around 1.1 millions, over a third of the entire urban population.

Otherwise, population was still fairly evenly distributed. The counties were still increasing in absolute numbers. The 'Celtic fringe' still accounted for nearly half (45 per cent) of United Kingdom population: Dublin (165,000) and Edinburgh (83,000) still followed London in the great towns league; Cork and Limerick were larger than most manufacturing towns. The complex organization of such regional centres reflected the predominant roles of local gentry, clergy, farmers, and professional people, and the result of decades of increasing trade.

Trade and Distribution

Trade more than industry still characterized the British economy. Continental towns were – or had only recently ceased to be – stringently controlled, their trade limited and taxed in complex and frustrating ways. The medieval gates of little German cities still swung shut at nightfall to keep 'foreigners' from their markets. But in Britain, by contrast, there were scarcely any impediments to internal commerce, while 'mercantilist' governments had positively encouraged the acquisition of 'treasure by foreign trade'. The eighteenth century had seen important changes. Seemingly perpetual war in the Channel and the attraction of large-scale smuggling, centred on the Isle of Man, had shifted commerce routes north. Liverpool rose on grain and slaves, then on cotton; Glasgow on tobacco and linen, then on cotton and engineering. Gradually, their entrepôt function was being changed by the opening up of efficient transport links to their hinterland, and its transformation by manufacturing industry.

Trade and distribution provided the central impulses for industrialization. No other European country had 30 per cent of its population in towns, to be fed, clothed, and warmed, or controlled such vast overseas markets. The institutions through which British merchants handled all this – which the law allowed, if not encouraged, them to set up – provided a framework in which increases in productivity could be translated into profit, credit, and further investment. At home, an expanding 'respectable class' provided a market for clothes, cutlery,

3. Sir David Wilkie, *The Irish Whiskey Still* of 1840. A romanticized view of rural Irish society before the famine, a period which, ironically, saw Ireland's greatest anti-liquor campaign under Father Mathew. Notice the good health of the peasants, and the potatoes in the lower left-hand corner

building materials, and china; this 'domestic' demand grew by some 42 per cent between 1750 and 1800. But in the same period the increase in export industries was over 200 per cent, most of this coming in the years after 1780.

Coal, Iron, and Textiles

Besides agriculture, three sectors were dominant – coal, iron, and textiles. The first two provided much of the capital equipment, infrastructure, and options for future development; but textiles made up over 50 per cent of exports by value in 1750, and over 60 per cent by 1800. Cotton, insignificant in 1750, was dominant with 39 per cent in 1810. Coal output doubled between 1750 and 1800, as steam pumps enabled deeper and more productive seams to be mined, and horse-worked railways bore coal ever-greater distances to water transport. Iron production, boosted by war demand, by the use of coal instead of charcoal for smelting, and by the perfecting in the 1780s of 'puddling' and 'rolling' wrought iron, rose by 200 per cent between 1788 and 1806. But textiles were the power which towed the glider of industrialization into the air.

Wool had always been England's great speciality, though linen, dominant on the Continent, was expanding under government patronage in Ireland and Scotland. Cotton rose largely through its adaptability to machine production, and the rapid increase in the supply of raw material that slavery in the American South made possible. The new machinery was primitive. But rising demand meant that resistance to its introduction by the labour force was overcome. John Kay's fly-shuttle loom (which doubled a weaver's output), destroyed when he tried to introduce it in the 1730s, was taken up in the 1770s, along with James Hargreaves's hand-operated spinning jenny (a multiple-spindle wheel) and Richard Arkwright's water-powered spinning frame. The last, and the great factories it required, spread from the Derbyshire valleys to Lancashire and Scotland. Before competition brought prices down – by two-thirds between 1784 and 1832 – huge fortunes could be made. Arkwright's shrewd exploitation of his patent rights brought him £200,000 and a baronetcy. Sir Robert Peel, calico printer and father of the future Tory premier, ended up by employing 15,000. Robert Owen reckoned that between 1799 and 1829 his New Lanark mills netted him and his partners £300,000 profit *after* paying a 5 per cent dividend. For some 20 years a modest prosperity extended, too, to the handloom weavers, before the introduction of power-looms and the flooding of the labour market with Irish immigrants and, after 1815, ex-servicemen. This turned the weavers' situation into one of the starkest tragedies of the age.

Engineering and Steam Power

Cotton technology spread to other textiles – speedily to Yorkshire worsteds, slowly to linen and wool. But it also boosted engineering and metal construction. Powerful and reliable machinery had to be built to drive thousands of spindles; mills – tinderboxes otherwise – had to be fireproofed with metal columns and joists. In 1770, Arkwright used millwrights and clockmakers to install his mainly wooden machinery at Cromford. But mill-design and machine-building soon became a specialized job, with waterwheels of up to 150 horsepower, complex spinning mules (a powered hybrid of the jenny and the frame, spinning very fine 'counts'), and the increased use of steam power.

James Watt patented his separate-condenser steam engine in 1774, and its rotative version in 1781. By 1800, cotton mills were its chief users, as it supplied reliable and continuous power for mule spinning. In its turn, the increasingly sophisticated technology required by the steam engine enhanced both its further application – to water transport in 1802, to locomotives in 1804 – and the development of the machine-tool industry, particularly associated with Henry Maudslay and his invention of the screw-cutting lathe. This (and its associated invention, the micrometer) made possible the absolutely accurate machining of parts. From now on, machines could reproduce themselves and be constructed in ever-greater complexity. The standards of the eighteenth-century clockmaker were no longer an expensive skill, but part of the conventional wisdom of mechanical engineering.

Transport

The creation of a transport infrastructure made for a golden age of civil engineering, too, as men such as James Brindley, John Smeaton, Thomas Telford, and John Rennie strove to exploit water-carriage and horsepower as efficiently as possible. In a parallel exploitation of wind power, sailing ships became so sophisticated that they remained

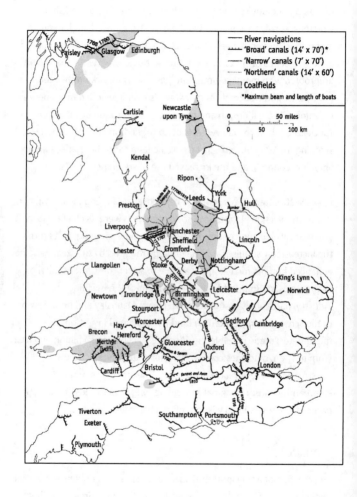

Map 1. The canal system in the early nineteenth century

competitive with steam until the 1880s. The country's awful roads were repaired and regulated, and in some cases built from scratch, by turnpike trusts, even by government. It took nearly a fortnight to travel from London to Edinburgh in 1745, two and a half days in 1796, and around 36 hours by coach or steamer in 1830.

Building on the steady growth of river navigation in the seventeenth century, 'dead-water' canals using pound locks were being built in Ireland in the 1730s. But it was the duke of Bridgewater's schemes to link Manchester with a local coalfield and Liverpool, 1760–71, that showed the importance of water transport for industrial growth. Bridgewater's engineer, Brindley, devised 'narrow' canals to prevent water loss in the 'dry' Midlands, and during the peace of 1764–72, when money was cheap, companies of gentry, merchants, manufacturers, and bankers managed to link all the major navigable rivers. Such private enterprise could pay, in the case of the Oxford canal, up to 30 per cent in dividend, but the average was about 8 per cent. The next boom, in the 1780s, pushed the system beyond what was commercially feasible, but Britain now had a transport network without parallel in Europe, while the unity of 'improvers', agricultural and industrial, in this cause overcame many of the barriers to further co-operation.

Chapter 3
Reform and Religion

The British government did not play, or wish to play, a positive role in industrialization; as the Corn Laws of 1815 were to show, neither did it abstain in the interests of *laissez-faire*. But increasingly it observed principles which were more or less systematic, and less unfavourable to industrial capitalists than they were to any other class – except, of course, landowners, who were frequently capitalists themselves in mining, transport, and property development. The axioms of William Blackstone and Edmund Burke: of continuity, the division of powers, the interpenetration of government, economy, and society – and above all the notion of government as a self-regulating mechanism – complemented the mechanics of classical economics, the discoveries of science, and even the cultivated deism of the upper classes.

Reform

But the ideal required renovation. Corruption and inefficiency had taken their toll at the time of the American War, and although the spectacle of mob violence – particularly in the Gordon Riots of 1780 – made respectable reformers more circumspect, reform was an admitted necessity. The messages of Adam Smith and John Wesley had, in their various ways, seen to that. The problem was, how could it be kept within constitutional bounds? Attempts such as the Association Movement to make politics more principled and symmetrical simply exposed the ramifications of 'interest' and downright corruption. The 'vast rotten borough' of Scotland, where only 4,000-odd electors returned 45 placemen MPs (only 1 man in 114 had the vote, compared with 1 in 7 in England), got its reward in the patronage distributed by its 'managers' the Dundas family, notably in the East India Company and the Admiralty. Ireland's 'free' Parliament, after 1782, was still an institution for which no Catholic could vote.

The opinion of the great manufacturing towns had to be articulated by pressure groups such as the General Chamber of Manufacturers, because of the gross maldistribution of political power. In 1801 the 700,000 people of Yorkshire had only 2 county and 26 borough MPs, while the 188,000 people of Cornwall had 2 county and 42 borough MPs. Dissenters and Catholics were allowed to vote after 1793 but could not sit in Parliament. On the other hand, so restricted was the impact of politics, and so expensive the business of getting on in it, that for some exclusion was a positive benefit. Although their overall numbers were in decline, the elaborate family relationships of the Quakers (who could not 'marry out' and remain in the sect) underpinned widely scattered enterprises ranging from iron- and lead-smelting works to banks and railways. The liberal-minded Unitarians, who 'believed in one God at most', were energetic leaders of provincial enlightenment in science and education.

The Evangelical Revival

Somewhat different was the Evangelical revival. Populist and traditional high church in origin, this drew inspiration from the religious heritage of the seventeenth century – exemplified by John Bunyan, and broadcast by John Wesley – and from the devotional literature of such as William Law. In contrast to 'Old Dissent' and Calvinist 'election', it stressed that grace was available to those who directed their life by biblical precept. It was respectable without being exclusive, ecumenical, and diffusely 'enthusiastic' (many who were to become its severest agnostic and high-church critics started as devout Evangelicals) – a faith of crisis, valid against atheistic revolution, unfeeling industrial relationships, and brutal personal behaviour. William Pitt drank and Charles James Fox gambled, but both were susceptible to the sort of pressure which well-placed Evangelicals could exert.

Methodism

The Evangelical revival was politically conservative, yet it soon flowed into peculiar channels. In 1795 the 'Society of Methodists' founded by Wesley left the Church of England because they could no longer accept conventional ordination. Tories they remained, but further Methodist groups such as the Primitives (who seceded in 1811) became more autonomous and more radical. Methodism was northern – 'the real religion of Yorkshire': elsewhere the Baptists and Congregationalists expanded in industrial towns whose elites were frequently Unitarian or Quaker. George Eliot described dissenting values in her 'political novel' about 1832, *Felix Holt* (1867):

> Here was a population not convinced that Old England was as good as possible; here were multitudinous men and women aware that their religion was not exactly the religion of their rulers, who might therefore be better than they were, and who, if better, might alter many things which now made the world perhaps more painful than it need be, and certainly more sinful.

'Vital religion' accomplished a religious revolution in Wales. In 1800 over 80 per cent of the population still adhered to the established Church whose mid-eighteenth-century missionary efforts, the 'circulating schools', had increased literacy (in Welsh) and enthusiasm beyond the point where it could sustain it. Into the vacuum flowed Calvinistic Methodism and the other nonconformist bodies; by 1851, Wales was 80 per cent chapel-going.

In Scotland, the established Presbyterian Church, which controlled education and poor relief, was practically a subordinate legislature. Controlled by the landowners and their worldly, liberal clergy, it was coming under increasing assault not only from independent Presbyterians, but from those, usually Evangelicals, who wished to transfer power to the congregations. In Ireland, the dissenting tradition was initially liberal, its leaders comparing their legal disadvantages with those of the Catholics. But the events of the 1790s, and the recrudescence of Evangelical fundamentalism, were ultimately to intensify the divide between the Protestant north-east and the rest of the country.

Chapter 4
The Wars Abroad

The French Revolution was greeted with general enthusiasm in Britain. At worst, it would weaken the old enemy; at best it would create another constitutional state. Charles James Fox, James Watt, Joseph Priestley, the young William Wordsworth, and Samuel Taylor Coleridge all celebrated it; Robert Burns was inspired to write 'Scots wha' hae' – which had obvious contemporary implications. Even the government was slow to echo Burke's severe censure in his *Reflections on the Revolution in France*, published in November 1790, while it still seemed a modest constitutional movement. Nonetheless, Burke expressed what the establishment felt, especially when Paris lurched leftwards in June 1791: remove customary deference and force would rule. Reform should be permitted only on terms which retained the basic political structure. Burke both attacked France and dramatized Blackstone's defence of the British political system. The establishment became really alarmed by the Anglo-American radical Tom Paine's reply, *The Rights of Man* (1791–2), with its bold proposals for individualist, democratic reform. Burke may himself have started what he tried to avoid. If the *Reflections* sold 18,000 copies in six months, *The Rights of Man* sold 200,000 – an incredible total for a society still only semi-literate. Pamphleteering had not demonstrated this range and impact since the Civil War.

War with France

The government was alarmed by two things above all – the impact of French notions of 'self-determination' on Britain's Low Country client states, and the contagion of ideas. The European monarchies, with even greater grounds for concern, abandoned the gentlemanly rules of eighteenth-century war in summer 1792 and treated the French as rabid dogs to be shot. The French reciprocated with the notion of war as a popular crusade: 'a nation in arms'. In Britain, the diplomatic threat worked on the political threat: warnings to France increased the conviction of some optimistic revolutionaries in Paris that war would lead to a British revolution. On 1 February 1793 France declared war.

Britain was unprepared. The army had only 45,000 men; scarcely a tenth of the battle-fleet could put to sea. Moreover, the war was quite different from earlier Anglo-French conflicts. The new style of army, the intensity of the revolutionary attack, the competence of France's new commanders: together these put Britain's allies in trouble from the start. By 1797 Austria had been knocked out and Britain stood alone against Bonaparte's Armée d'Angleterre.

Three things preoccupied the government in those early war years: the threat of invasion, the cost of the war, and the problem of combating internal dissension. The French made three invasion attempts, once via Wales and twice via Ireland. A landing in Pembrokeshire in 1797 found no support, but in autumn 1798, after the bloody suppression by the British of Presbyterian and Catholic rebels (30,000 may have died), a force under General Humbert landed in Mayo and was quickly defeated. The government hoped to defend the mainland by fortifying the coast with Martello towers, embodying the Militia (the home defence force), and extending the Militia Acts to Scotland and Ireland. All this gave ceaseless headaches to the part-time local officials involved. As subsidies to allies were running into tens of millions by 1795, taxation had to be increased radically and included, after 1799, the innovation of an income tax levied at 2s. (10p) in the pound. Finally the government acted drastically against groups which sought peace or solidarity with the French. 'Pitt's reign of terror' in 1793–4, supplemented by the local activities of magistrates, industrialists, and patriotic societies, destroyed many of the radical societies. The repression was particularly fierce in Scotland, where Lord Braxfield's brutal Doric humour arbitrarily upheld 'the most perfect constitution ever created'.

Braxfield's sarcasms – on being told by one of his victims that Jesus was a reformer, his reply was 'Muckle he made o' that. He waur hangit tae!' – symbolized the end of the upper-class liberalism of the Scottish Enlightenment. Thirty years of fairly constant repression followed, wielded by Pitt's Scottish lawyer allies, the Dundas family.

In Ireland, the reversal was even more drastic. War led Pitt to pressurize the Irish Parliament into granting Catholics voting rights in 1793, in an attempt to win them from enthusiasm for 'godless' France. But the non-sectarian radicalism of the United Irishmen rapidly grew. By 1798, it was countered in Ulster by the ultra-Protestant Orange Lodges and by the local violence of a Catholic peasantry bitterly resentful at Protestant privileges, and in part influenced by French-trained priests imbued with revolutionary ideals. Shortly before Humbert landed there was a vicious, though short-lived, outburst in Wicklow, enough to convince the Protestant ascendancy of its isolation. In 1800 Ireland's ruling class followed the example of the Scots in 1707, and entered into political union with England.

The Effects of War

Apart from the brief interlude of 1801–3, the 'wars abroad' lasted until 1815. By then, Britain had spent £1,500 million on war; yet the effects were ambiguous and curiously limited. The war was soon erased from popular memory. Britain was an armed camp for much of the time: there were constant drafts into the militia, and at any stage about a sixth of the adult male population may have been under arms. Compared with France, few of these actually served abroad, although many – around 210,000 – died. What was in France a demographic setback – its population increased by 32 per cent, 1800–50, compared with Britain's 50 per cent – had a different, smaller impact on Britain. Yet British naval supremacy was never challenged after 1805, and through blockades it destroyed much of French industry, whose most dynamic sectors were based on the trading ports.

Adam Smith had written that war would distort demand and create a 'seller's market' among certain types of labour. It proceeded to do so. The iron trade boomed not only in its traditional base of the West Midlands, but in central Scotland and also in South Wales, where Merthyr Tydfil expanded twenty-fold in population between 1780 and 1820 – a raw, remote city (accessible, incredibly, by canal) in a country whose largest mid-eighteenth-century town, Carmarthen, had contained scarcely 4,000 people. As blockade throttled its rivals, Britain's ever more commanding lead in textiles reached the stage where its manufacturers were clothing French armies. The huge naval dockyards of Chatham, Portsmouth, and Devonport were further expanded and became pioneers of mass production. Their creations, the sailing warships, were dramatically improved; steam power, when it took over in the 1850s, was almost a lesser revolution.

The navy, in fact, typified many of government's problems. The wretched condition of the sailors provoked mutinies at Spithead and the Nore in 1797. These had little political content; the mutineers, however aggrieved, remained overwhelmingly patriotic. They were dealt with by a mixture of coercion and concession – as indeed were the well-organized dockyard workers. Elsewhere, government reacted ambiguously to attempts to remedy working-class distress. The Combination Laws of 1799 treated trade unions like revolutionary societies and outlawed them; government also successfully opposed attempts to secure legal minimum wages and restore older industrial relationships, even when these were backed by manufacturers (on the whole smaller ones). Such measures, and the depressions which resulted from the diversion of investment into government funds and the trade war, ensured that average real wages stagnated between 1790 and 1814. Yet the relatively generous poor relief scales adopted by many rural parishes after the 1790s – the so-called Speenhamland system – continued a traditional entitlement to relief, and undoubtedly mitigated even sharper social conflicts.

Results Overseas

For most of the war Britain avoided European involvement, and paid subsidies instead to the members of the various coalitions it assembled, first against revolutionary France, then against Napoleon. This was simply a refinement of the mercenary principles of eighteenth-century wars. Only between 1811 and 1814, when Britain sent its own troops to the Peninsula, did its army take on a European role. The gains in other areas, however, were immense; Britain's hold over India was strengthened, and it achieved effective dominance, through Singapore, of the Dutch East Indies; it conquered Ceylon between 1795 and 1816, took over South Africa from the Dutch, and established a claim on Egypt. Informally, Britain secured a trading hegemony over the former Spanish colonies of Central and South America.

Although Britain was victorious, the war's imprint on Europe was predominantly French. Wherever Napoleon's armies went, they left (or their opponents copied) the laws, the measurements, the administration – and above all the nationalistic ethos – of the revolution. The map had been totally changed. Before 1789, Britain had been part of a Continental community. David Hume and Adam Smith were as much at home in Paris as they were in Edinburgh, and rather more, perhaps, than they were in London. After 1815, Britain, despite the economic progress which attracted hundreds of foreign visitors, remained at a distance from European life.

4. The battle of Waterloo, 18 June 1815: the death of General Picton. This shows the highly formal nature of infantry warfare in the age of the muzzle-loading 'Brown Bess' musket, where drill and discipline had to compensate for inefficient weapons

Results at Home

At home, war and depression polarized political ideas into 'revolutionary' and 'loyalist'. 'Pitt's reign of terror', patriotic societies, and church-and-king mobs pushed democratic thinkers, earlier commonplace enough, either into obscurity or into alliance with genuinely oppressed groups like the Irish or the working class. The 'Jacobin tradition' became as sensitive to industrial and economic change as it had been to the 'evils' of established government. A diffuse, volatile blend of everything from anarchism to religious millenarianism, it continued to mark working-class movements up to and including Chartism.

The Benthamites

Paradoxically, however, the relentlessly practical approach of the governing elite, and the role of repression in exalting state power over contractual ideas of politics, conjured up its own radical rival. Evangelicalism, in the hands of William Wilberforce and the Clapham Sect, aimed at converting the elite; but so too did the reiterated schemes of Jeremy Bentham, a wealthy lawyer who believed, more or less, that society could be governed through a set of self-evident principles analogous to those of economics. Of these, the most easily grasped was 'utilitarianism' – that social action should aim at producing 'the greatest good for the greatest number'. The sworn foe to all ideals of 'social contract', Bentham opposed the French Revolution, and tried to interest successive British governments in his schemes, particularly of law and prison reform. He was probably more successful than he thought, but frustrations drove him towards the democratic reformers and by 1815 he was supporting universal suffrage.

The 'philosophic radicals', as Bentham's disciples were called, offered the combination of institutional reform with political continuity – and, after 1815, offered it to both sides, as they built up a following of moderate working-class leaders. From this stemmed both a centralized pattern of State action, and a theory of public intervention, which remained powerfully influential for the rest of the century.

Benthamite theory saw local authorities raising rates and taking executive action in appropriately sized districts. They would be supervised by salaried inspectors reporting to a central board. 'Old corruption' and popular profligacy would thus be supposedly checked; local responsibility would be retained. But, in fact, the officials were dominant. Bentham and his acolytes, the Mills, father and son, and Edwin Chadwick, may have been converted to democracy, but they were reluctant to let the people's representatives do more than veto the officials' actions. Not surprisingly, their most spectacular successes were gained in British India.

The Law

Law had shifted into a class pattern. Working men, accustomed to fight disabilities in the courts, lost traditional rights and had their independent action constrained. The alarm of the propertied classes gave teeth to hitherto ineffective sanctions. The 'making of the English working class' was, at least in part, a reaction to a combination of war, industrialization, and repression: it meant a hostility to inequitable law. There was little respect for 'the Thing' (the undeclared confederacy of the rich to exhaust the poor) in William Cobbett; practical ignorance of it in Robert Owen. Even the Benthamites thought the legal establishment a 'vast sinister interest'. Although ultimately only the Irish stood out against it, the triumph of the rule of law, like Waterloo, proved 'a damned close-run thing'. It was probably only possible because popular expectations of it endured long enough to be sustained by a new wave of constitutional agitation.

Chapter 5
Roads to Freedom

Men of England, wherefore plough
For the Lords who lay ye low?
Wherefore weave with toil and care
The rich robes your tyrants wear?

. . .

Shrink to your cellars, holes and cells;
In halls ye deck another dwells.
Why shake the chains ye wrought? Ye see
The steel ye tempered glance on ye.

Shelley, *To the Men of England*

The post-war Tory government after 1815 encountered a new set of literary radicals. Coleridge and Wordsworth, gathered to the bosom of the forces of order, were succeeded by Lord Byron and Percy Bysshe Shelley. Lord Liverpool's administration of 1812–27 was in fact a pretty bourgeois affair, made up of minor gentry, the sons of doctors and merchants, and even (in the case of George Canning), an actress. Although condemned as reactionary – which some of its members certainly were – it sat edgily on the right centre. It was liberal (by the standards of Restoration Europe) abroad, and conciliatory at home. But it inherited a fearsome post-war slump and racking industrial tensions, on top of a war debt to be paid for, and demobilized servicemen to be settled. It was scarcely aided by an able Whig opposition, which lacerated it through the medium of the new literary reviews, and a rich culture of popular protest, from the 'unstamped' newspapers of Henry Hetherington and Richard Carlile to the bucolic radicalism of William Cobbett and the visionary millenarianism of William Blake. The landed interest pressed for, and obtained, the maintenance of subsidy on grain through the Corn Law of 1815; this probably staved off, for over a decade, discontent among those of the working population who tilled the land. But it was all at a cost. Even more than in 1811–12, the threat to order came from the new industrial towns, where the end of the post-war boom caused widespread unemployment and a steep fall in wages. The consciousness of the workers, more of their *industrial* than of their class position, had steadily sharpened since 1800, and the local representatives of government, manufacturers and justices of the peace, felt their isolation acutely.

London and the Provinces

Do the fears that these gentry frequently expressed – of Jacobin mobs baying at their gates – and the explicitly revolutionary ideas of some leaders of the working classes add up to a real threat to overthrow the regime, which was only narrowly averted? They might have done, had action been co-ordinated, had a common economic cause existed to bind industrial workers to the parliamentary radicals and the skilled trades of the capital, and had the governing classes really lost their nerve. But this would have been very difficult to achieve. London was not an 'absolute' capital like Paris; there were few vital levers of power to be grasped had the London radicals mobilized *en masse*.

London did not move with the provinces. The parliamentary opposition disowned and deprecated violence, and the Home Office under its repressive head, Viscount Sidmouth, and his local agents cowed resistance – but at a price. The climax came in Manchester on 16 August 1819, when the local magistracy ordered the yeomanry to apprehend speakers at a huge but peaceful reform demonstration in St Peter's Fields. The soldiers turned on the crowd and 11 were killed at 'Peterloo'. Both the desire of radicals for revenge and the penetration of the radical movement by government spies and *agents provocateurs* were responsible for further outbreaks in the following year – a weavers' rising in Scotland and the 'Cato Street conspiracy' to assassinate the Cabinet in London. Repression – the gallows and transportation – was sharp, savage, and effective, but in the long term it strengthened constitutional resistance and steadily discredited the government.

Social Peril and Salvation

The government itself looked askance at unbound industrialization. Moving towards free trade, systematic administration, and a reformed penal code, it still depended on the agricultural interest, and feared further working-class violence. Sir Walter Scott, its supporter, regretted the shift of industry to the towns, since he believed that in country mills the manufacturer 'exercised a salutary influence over men depending on and intimately connected with him and his prospects'. He probably had Robert Owen and New Lanark in mind. Propagandizing for self-governing industrial communities, Owen wanted to put a brake on industry and, through spade-cultivation, make agriculture again a great employer. His 'new moral world' fitted into the atmosphere of social peril and utopian salvation which had been pervasive since the end of the war:

> The Strongest Poison ever known
> Came from Caesar's Laurel Crown.
> Nought can deform the Human Race
> Like to the Armour's iron brace.
> When Gold & Gems adorn the Plow
> To peaceful Arts shall Envy bow.

Artisans did not need to understand the artisan genius William Blake's cosmology to appreciate the message. The future must have seemed to many as apocalyptic as the huge but minutely detailed and didactic paintings of John Martin, which had a great vogue as engravings in the mid-1820s.

The Political Battle

The Whig contribution to the political battle was, however, effective enough. In 1820 George IV's attempt to divorce his consort led to the royal family's dirty linen being washed in the courts. Henry Brougham, a leading contributor to the *Edinburgh Review*, championed Queen Caroline (not the most promising of martyrs) against king and ministry, to the plaudits of the public. Then in August 1822 Castlereagh, who as foreign secretary had managed to extricate Britain from the conservative powers represented in Metternich's Congresses, killed himself. The way was open for the more liberal side of the Liverpool government to show itself.

Castlereagh's successor at the Foreign Office, George Canning, sided with the American president Monroe in 1823 in guaranteeing the new republics of South America – and incidentally confirmed Britain's privileged access to a vast new market. Two years later the ministry repealed the anti-radical Six Acts of 1819 and anti-trade union legislation, and in 1826 it ended the 'management' of Scotland by the Dundases. The duke of Wellington's administration passed Catholic Emancipation in 1829. It bowed to Daniel O'Connell's expert management of Irish public opinion, and to the threat of a national uprising when O'Connell was elected as MP for County Clare in 1828 but, as a Catholic, was debarred from taking his seat.

Parliamentary Reform

Only parliamentary reform remained to be implemented, but here a direct party issue was involved. Pressure groups – the trade unions, the

Scots, the Irish – could be bought off with judicious concessions. Reform, however, would mean a triumph for the Whigs, with all that meant in terms of parliamentary command and patronage. In 1828 the duke had dug his heels in, under pressure from his 'Ultras', but in the following year they parted from him over Catholic Emancipation. Meanwhile in the country agitation grew, and the Whigs did not scruple to encourage their radical rivals. Pressure rose to a peak after the Whigs under Earl Grey and Lord John Russell won the election which the death of George IV occasioned in 1830. When their Reform Bill was rejected by the Lords, well-organized 'Political Unions' held monster rallies in the cities; rioters attacked Nottingham Castle and the bishop's palace in Bristol, both seats of anti-Reform peers; in Merthyr riots were followed by the execution of a workers' leader, Dic Penderyn. In April 1832 the Lords gave way – by nine votes – much to the relief of Grey's government, which had shown its otherwise conservative nature by the brutal suppression of farm labourers' discontent – the 'Captain Swing' riots – in southern England.

Chapter 6
Coping with Reform

Despite the near-revolutionary nature of the reform agitation, the act of 1832 incorporated the most potentially troublesome sectors of industrial and commercial power, but did little more. Scotland's electorate shot up from 4,579 to 64,447 (a 1,407 per cent increase), but that of Ireland increased by only 21 per cent; 41 large English towns – including Manchester, Bradford, and Birmingham – got representation for the first time, but the average size of an English borough electorate – and these returned almost half (324) of the total of 658 MPs – remained under 900. The 349 electors of Buckingham still returned as many MPs as the 4,172 electors of Leeds. England, with 54 per cent of the population, continued to return 71 per cent of the Commons. Before 1832 it had returned 74 per cent. 'Virtual representation', of interests rather than people, remained a principle, and Parliament continued to be dominated by the landed interest for almost a further half-century.

The Working Class

Some conservatives now feared a Benthamite assault on the aristocracy and the Church. But there were few doctrinaires in Parliament, and the reforming zeal of the Whigs rapidly waned. Humanitarians got their way in 1833 with the abolition of slavery in the British Empire and the regulation of children's work in textile factories by the Factory Inspectorate. The Poor Law Amendment Act of 1834, which its architect

Edwin Chadwick saw as the basis of a systematic and economical reconstruction of English local government, remained, however, an isolated monument – as much hated by the people as were its symbols, the gaunt Union workhouses or 'bastilles'.

The Times, too, was loud in abuse of the New Poor Law, feeling perhaps that philosophical radicalism had gone far enough. For 1834 was a traumatic year. Ireland was quiet for once, the Whigs edging towards an understanding with O'Connell, which lasted for the rest of the decade, but on the mainland the 'alternative society' of the still-inchoate working class reached its apogee. The growth of trade unions, led by men such as John Doherty; the arguments of the 'unstamped' press; the frustration of radicals with the Reform Act; the return to politics of Robert Owen – all combined to produce a project for a Grand National Consolidated Trades Union which would destroy the capitalist system through a 'grand national holiday' or general strike. After this, society would be reorganized on a co-operative basis, with money values calculated in terms of hours of labour performed. Government counterattacked in March with the victimization of six Dorset labourers – the 'Tolpuddle Martyrs'; the GNCTU undertook too many protests and strikes, which its organizers could not co-ordinate. Owen pulled out in August and effectively brought the movement to an end. On 16 October Parliament accidentally burned down; six months earlier this might have appeared more than simply symbolic.

Local Government Reform

The Whig triumph really came with local government reform. Scottish burgh councils, hitherto self-elected, were put under a ratepayer franchise in 1833; reform of the English towns followed two years later. In the larger towns, Whigs and radicals came into the fruits of office, and by and large stayed there. But the government was now badly split. In November 1834 the Tories, now under Peel and more or less pledged to work within the framework of reform, took office. A false dawn, this:

the Whigs were back in April 1835, but under the deeply conservative Viscount Melbourne. When they fell from power in 1841 Peel seemed more acutely to reflect the spirit of gradualist reform, an outlook shared with the young queen's serious-minded consort, Albert of Saxe-Coburg-Gotha.

The Anti-Corn Law League

Peel, however, was threatened from two sides. Manufacturers, concerned at falling profits, demanded lower wages, and believed that they could only get them if the price of bread was reduced (bread was the staple diet of the working class – they ate about five pounds of it per head per week). This could only be done by permitting the free import of grain, in other words by repealing the Corn Law of 1815. Radicals, frustrated by Whig backsliding, climbed on to the bandwagon and grabbed the reins. Richard Cobden, a none-too-successful cotton merchant with transatlantic interests, John Bright, a Quaker carpet manufacturer from Rochdale, and James Wilson, the Scottish journalist who founded the *Economist* in 1843, became leading figures in the Anti-Corn Law League, inaugurated at a meeting in Manchester in October 1838. The League both represented, and in part created, the commercial-minded individualistic middle class – what the Germans called (and still call) 'Manchestertum'. By petitions, demonstrations, the mobilization of nonconformity, and the imaginative use of the new penny post, it created a widespread animus against the territorial aristocracy, and against Peel himself.

Peel had, in fact, followed most of the precepts of political economy in his public finance: duties on imports were drastically reduced, the Bank of England reorganized, railway promotion allowed to have its free enterprise head (despite the predilection of William Gladstone, the President of the Board of Trade, for outright nationalization). But the Leaguers acted with the fury of the desperate. They realized that their prosperity was borne on the back of an increasingly mutinous labour force. An extremely unorthodox Manchester cotton-master, the young German Friedrich Engels, watched the successive waves of discontent breaking against the mill-walls, and prophesied: 'The moment the workers resolve to be bought and sold no longer, when, in the determination of the value of labour, they take the part of men possessed of a will as well as of working power, at that moment the whole Political Economy of today is at an end.' Engels's chosen instruments were the ultimate in economic depressions, and the power of the organized working class expressed in Chartism.

Chartism

'I cares nothing about politics neither; but I'm a chartist', a London scavenger told Henry Mayhew, the pioneer social investigator, in 1848. The People's Charter, with its celebrated six points – manhood suffrage, the ballot, equal electoral districts, abolition of property qualifications for MPs, payment for MPs, and annual Parliaments – achieved the same immediate impact as the French Revolution and O'Connell's campaigns in Ireland. But this only gave a superficial and episodic unity to an immensely complex, highly localized movement. Formally it was ultra-democratic (although only as far as men were concerned – a proposal for female suffrage was an early casualty). In its most dramatic nationwide phase it was also short-lived, lasting from 1838 to 1842. But organization, and heterodoxy, bubbled away in the regions, influenced by the local economic predicaments, political traditions, and the character of the leaders. The division between 'physical-' and 'moral-force' leaders was complicated by attitudes to the established parties, the drink question, Ireland, property, and education. In Scotland and the English Midlands, leadership came from small tradesmen with a sprinkling of business and professional men. In Yorkshire it was militant, following heavy unemployment and the impact of the New Poor Law, but participated with the Tories in their campaign for factory reform. The 'frontier towns' of industrial Wales had already seen plenty of 'collective bargaining by riot', so it was possibly not surprising that a

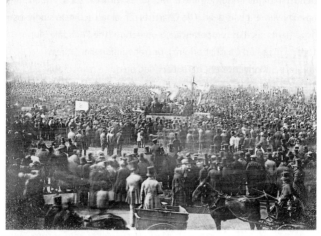

5. The last great Chartist rally, Kennington Common, 10 April 1848. Although engravings after this daguerrotype have often been reproduced, the original remained, undiscovered, in the royal archives until the 1970s. It bears out the French political writer Tocqueville's comment that it was all but impossible to tell British classes apart by dress, and shows the almost exclusively male character of mid-century radicalism

huge protest demonstration at Newport, on 4 November 1839, ended as a bloody confrontation with the Military. Fourteen were killed, but subsequent trials led to transportation to Tasmania, not the gallows.

Peel was more humane and tactful than Melbourne in 1831 or Liverpool in 1819, and his policy succeeded. The economic boom of 1843 and 1844 sapped Chartism; its last revival in 1848 reflected the agony of Ireland rather than the ambitions of the English artisans, or any desire to emulate events in Europe. Late Chartism was more experimental and variegated, as well as more Irish. Feargus O'Connor projected land settlement schemes, and Owenite and socialist ideas came back, along with ideas culled from European revolutionaries, many of whom ended up as exiles in Britain. But however fascinating intellectually the friendship of Julian Harney and Ernest Jones with Marx and Engels, the mass movement was dead. Old Chartists remained active in single-issue movements such as temperance, co-operation (the Rochdale Pioneer store of 1844 had Chartist origins), or trade unionism. Others emigrated. Many former Chartists ended up quite respectably integrated into mid-Victorian local government and the new provincial press.

Chapter 7
'Unless the Lord Build the City . . .'

In 1832 an appalling cholera epidemic, sweeping through Europe from the Middle East, killed probably 31,000 in Britain; in 1833 Parliament voted a £30,000 grant to elementary education, and John Keble preached at Oxford on 'national apostasy'. These events merely coincided with political reform – Parliament spent more time and money on the stables of Windsor Castle than on the education grant – but were important determinants of the direction that subsequent state action took, and the way in which the early Victorians rationalized their social position.

Housing and Sanitation

Cholera dramatized the problem of rapid urban growth, though its impact could be as deadly in the countryside. The new industrial towns were small in area, and densely packed, as walking to work was universal. Urban land usage accorded with economic power: the numerically tiny property-owning class, possibly less than 5 per cent of the population in a cotton town, often occupied 50 per cent of the land area. Working people lived where factories, roads, canals, and, later, railways allowed them to. The results were squalid – nineteenth-century towns smoked and stank – and, for the workers, expensive in terms of both rent and human life. A tolerable house might take a quarter of a skilled man's weekly income, and few families were ever in a position to afford this. As a result, not only did slums multiply in the old inner-city area – the rookeries of London, the cellar-dwellings of Liverpool and Manchester, the 'lands' of the Scottish burghs, 'China' in Merthyr Tydfil – but new regionally specific types of slum were created by landlords and speculative builders – the 'back-to-backs' of Yorkshire and the tiny 'room and kitchen' or 'single-end' flats in which 70 per cent of Glasgow families lived by 1870.

If housing was bad, sanitation was worse. Better-off citizens could combine to create commissions to provide water and sewerage, light the streets, and provide some sort of policing, but if anything, this worsened the plight of their poorer neighbours. A middle-class area's new water-closets all too often drained into the working class's water supply.

Health Reform

Epidemics were the working class's revenge. Surrounded by masses of the very poor in the shape of servants and tradespeople (whom they usually ignored), the wealthy suddenly became intensely vulnerable. A. C. Tait, a future archbishop of Canterbury, for example, lost five of his seven children to scarlet fever in Carlisle in 1856. In 1831 the government forced local notables to serve on temporary boards of health, in order to combat cholera. In 1840 Edwin Chadwick, concerned at the numbers driven into pauperism by the death of the breadwinner and ill-health, conducted on behalf of the Poor Law Commissioners an *Inquiry into the Sanitary Condition of the Labouring Population*, published in 1842. As a result of this, and subsequent agitation, not to speak of the threat of another cholera outbreak, an act of 1848 gave municipalities powers to set up local boards of health, subject to three public health commissioners, among them Chadwick himself. Besides the Benthamites, other forces had been mobilized – some Chartists and radicals, but probably more Tories, professional men, and philanthropists. Exemplifying the movement as a whole was Lord

Ashley. The future earl of Shaftesbury could be a prejudiced low-church Tory – Macaulay referred to his style as 'the bray of Exeter Hall' – but he inherited William Wilberforce's skills at manipulating public, and elite, opinion to secure effective government intervention. In the 1840s and 1850s these skills were used to help miners, factory hands, poor emigrants, and slum-dwellers. Some have argued that administrative reform took on a dynamic of its own, independent of both parliamentary action and ideology. 'The Tory interpretation of history' (as this view has somewhat unfairly been called) contrasted the power of officials – 'the men on the spot' – and enthusiasts like Ashley virtually to create their own laws, with Parliament's indifference to social conditions.

But this is only a partial explanation of the reform process. Standards of conduct among officials varied from department to department, and between individuals. Some were dedicated to the point of self-sacrifice, others reflected the easy-going ethos of a civil service still recruited by patronage. Anthony Trollope, as a senior official of the Post Office, still found time to hunt twice a week, and to turn out a steady 1.7 novels per annum – one of which, *The Three Clerks* (1857), gives an engaging picture of a backwater of the unreformed civil service, and Trollope's own sour observations on its reformers.

As this was the golden age both of 'local self-government' and of professional evolution, the strongest initiatives came from the great cities, and from a new generation of largely Scottish-trained doctors, who were making the transition from lowly surgeon-apothecaries into a self-governing profession. Liverpool appointed the first medical officer of health in 1847; the City of London, a 'square mile' rich in every variety of social peril, appointed the dynamic Dr John Simon a year later. By 1854 the appointment of Medical Officers of Health was compulsory, and proved critical in getting the cities not only to undertake major water, drainage, and slum clearance schemes, but to ensure that regulations on building and overcrowding were enforced.

Education

The new industrial society brought into question the organization of education. Opinions on this differed: the Evangelical Hannah More believed that to inculcate religion but preserve order, children should learn to read but not write. Adam Smith, fearing the intellectually stultifying impact of the division of labour on the working class, sought to mitigate it by state education. Although this existed in Scotland, as a result of the Calvinist reformation of the Kirk, there was no English equivalent. Before the 1800s, there were grammar schools, frequently of pre-Reformation origin, independent or 'adventure' schools, and charity schools. These varied enormously in quality, and could never accommodate an expanding and youthful population, let alone service the new urban areas and improve standards. Around 1800, however, opinion – including even that of George III – swung towards education as a prophylactic against revolution – partly through the appearance of new, cheap, and thus seductive forms of teaching. The 'monitorial' systems of Joseph Lancaster and Andrew Bell, whereby senior pupils learned lessons by rote and then instructed their juniors, led directly to the foundation of the British and Foreign Schools Society in 1808, and the National Society in 1811. These two attempts at national coverage, however, coincided with the exacerbation of hostilities between their respective sponsors, the nonconformists and the established Church; religious animus continued to take precedence over educational criteria for nearly a century.

Religious antagonisms in the reform of the endowed, or 'public', schools were internal to Anglicanism, and less fierce. The schools' condition, peculiarly wretched in the last years of the eighteenth century, had, improved even before the radical Broad-Churchman Thomas Arnold began his career at Rugby in 1829. His reforms, in fact, paralleled the essentially conservative political settlement of 1832, but lasted far longer. A 'liberal education' (Latin and Greek) remained dominant among those destined for the universities, but it was elevated from a totally meaningless ritual for young aristocrats into the subject-matter of competitive advancement, through scholarships and, at Oxford and Cambridge, college fellowships, for middle-class boys. Their goals were the prizes of subsidized entry into the professions, but their function was more profound: to act as bell-wethers guiding other boys from the commercial middle class into a sanitized version of the values of the territorial aristocracy. By the time he died in 1842, Arnold was being imitated at the other older public schools, and the movement proceeded, aided by the expansion of the railway system and, in 1857, by Thomas Hughes's remarkably successful *Tom Brown's Schooldays*.

Christian Socialism

The remodelling of the public schools provided a paradigm for a new generation of reformers, many of whom had been educated there. Unlike the Benthamites, they developed no highly integrated programme, but rather sought to convert institutions accessible only to the aristocracy and the Anglican clergy to serve the whole of society. This ideal of 'nationalization' with its corollary, the 'incorporation' of the working class into 'political society', was expressed in 1848 by the Christian Socialist followers of F. D. Maurice – including Tom Hughes – in their attempt to make the Church of England an arbiter between capital and labour. They were not alone. In Bradford William Edward Forster, a young radical woollen manufacturer, formerly a Quaker, wrote:

> Unless some concessions be made to these masses, and unless all classes strive earnestly to keep them better fed, first or last there will be a convulsion; but I believe the best political method of preventing it is by the middle class sympathising with the operatives, and giving themselves power to oppose their unjust claims by helping them in those which are reasonable.

Forster's wife was the daughter of Arnold of Rugby, the sister of Matthew Arnold, inspector of schools and poet. The 'intellectual aristocracy' of high thinking and moderate reform was already shifting from Evangelical religion to political intervention.

Oxford Movement and Broad Church

Arnold, the public schools, and most of the politicians belonged to the Broad Church or liberal Anglican tradition, whose principles envisaged the Church as partner of the State, a relationship to which theological doctrine was strictly subordinate. The Evangelicals exalted religious sanctions, but their simple theology was being corroded by liberal assaults, which seemed to reach a climax with the Reform Act of 1832. Clergymen feared that a tide of Benthamite, and hence atheistic, reform would be unleashed; John Keble in an Oxford sermon declared a clerical resistance which would be founded on the apostolic traditions of the Church of England. 'Tractarianism', or the Oxford Movement, did not oppose liberalism through social reform or through 'high-church' ceremonial. It was a conservative, intellectual appeal to Anglican tradition. After 12 years it split, in 1845, when some of its leaders, including John Henry Newman (partly in reaction to low-church persecution, partly out of sheer intellectual conviction), decided that nothing separated them from Rome, and 'went over'. Although its enemies forecast otherwise, the Oxford Movement served to strengthen the spirit of Anglicanism both through devout laymen such as W. E. Gladstone and through its influence on religious education and architecture.

The Broad Church, being posited on a more sociological appreciation of religion, was in difficulties when it appeared that less than a fifth of the English attended their parish church. The unique religious Census of 1851 showed that only about 35 per cent of the English population went to Sunday service, and – although there were intense regional variations here – half of these 'sat under' dissenting ministers. In 1848 and after the Broad Church Christian Socialists tried energetically to reach out to working men, but for every working man convinced by the theology of the group's leader, Maurice, ten were impressed by the novels of his colleague Charles Kingsley, and many more helped practically by the work of J. M. Ludlow for the trade unions and E. V. Neale for the infant co-operative movement.

Anglicans at least possessed a tradition, wealth, and breadth of manoeuvre denied to the nonconformists. Sectionally divided and always treated with suspicion by the ruling classes, several of their leaders – notably Jabez Bunting of the Methodist Conference – tried to integrate themselves through their conservatism. Political radicalism tended to be the hallmark of rural or mining area Dissenters – the change in South Wales was particularly drastic – or of urban elites such as the Unitarians or the Quakers. Only in the 1850s, after the success of the Corn Law campaign, did dissent begin to flex its muscles, align itself with the Liberal Party, and demand either improvements in its own civic status or – in the programme of the 'Liberation Society' (founded in 1844) – the dismantling of the established Church. Organized dissent came to play a major – and troublesome – institutional role within Liberalism, but it was a wasting asset, as the steady trickle of wealthy nonconformists over to the Church of England showed.

In Scotland the controversy over patronage came to a head in the 'ten years' conflict' of 1833–43, which ended with the 'Disruption' of the established Kirk and the creation of a new independent 'Free Church'. The secular role of the Kirk rapidly crumbled – a statutory Poor Law was enacted in 1845 – but religious politics continued to obsess the Scots middle class for the rest of the century.

Chapter 8

'The Ringing Grooves
of Change'

The 1840s remained, however, a decade of crisis, even in terms of classical economics. British industry was still dominated by textiles, and the market for them was both finite and subject to increasing competition from America and Europe. The industry was over-capitalized, and the adoption of each new invention meant that the return on capital decreased; each commercial depression was steeper and longer lasting than the last. Real wages increased only slowly, probably not sufficiently to counter the precipitate decline of the handwork trades and the high marginal costs of urban life. To Marx, surveying Britain through the descriptions of his mill-owning friend Engels, this was all part of one pattern. Capitalism was doomed to choke on its own surplus accumulations of capital; its increasingly underpaid labourers would, in the next economic depression, rise decisively against it. He would have echoed Shelley's challenge:

Rise like Lions after slumber
In unvanquishable number –
Shake your chains to earth like dew
Which in sleep had fallen on you –
Ye are many – they are few.

In the 1840s events in Ireland seemed to bring the revolution perceptibly nearer. The potato blight of 1845, 1846, and 1848 destroyed the basis of the country's population growth; between 1845 and 1850 up to a million died of the consequences of malnutrition; two million emigrated between 1845 and 1855. The poor Irish immigrant, prepared to work for wages far below the English norm, had already been seen as an explosive force; Carlyle had written in *Chartism* (1839): 'Every man who will take the statistic spectacles off his nose, and look, may discern in town or country. . . [that] the condition of the lower multitude of English labourers approximates more and more to the Irish competing with them in all markets. . .' That this did not happen was substantially due to a dramatic industrial development which simultaneously soaked up surplus supplies of labour and capital and transformed them into a new and more varied economy. Its principal – and psychologically most spectacular – instrument was the railway.

The Railways

Railways of various primitive types had since the early seventeenth century carried coal from mine to port or river; by 1800 there were perhaps 200 miles of horse-worked track scattered throughout the country, built to various gauges and patterns, with wooden and later with iron rails. Cast iron was used from the 1770s, wrought iron 'edge-rail' – much more reliable – from the 1790s. Steam traction then appeared in two forms: stationary low-pressure engines dragged wagons up inclines, and light high-pressure 'locomotive' engines moved themselves on the rails. In 1804, Richard Trevithick demonstrated the locomotive in Wales, and it was soon adopted in the northern coalfield, where 'viewers' like George Stephenson were building large-capacity edge-railways whose demands stretched the capabilities of horse traction, as coal production doubled between 1800 and 1825. Throughout Britain by 1830, 375 miles of line, authorized by Parliament, had been built.

The commercial boom of the mid-1820s gave the next boost, with the promotion of the Liverpool and Manchester Railway. Cotton production

	Before 1838
+—+—+	1838 – 48
	1849 – 72
·········	1873 – 1914

Edinburgh

Glasgow

Berwick on Tweed

Newcastle upon Tyne

Carlisle

Stockton

Darlington

Lancaster

York

Leeds

Holyhead

Liverpool

Manchester

Doncaster

Crewe

Derby

Nottingham

Norwich

Birmingham

Peterboro'

Rugby

Cambridge

Gloucester

Oxford

Swansea

Bristol

Swindon

London

Cardiff

Southampton

Dover

Exeter

Brighton

Weymouth

Portsmouth

0		50 miles
0	50	100 km

Map 2. Railways, 1825–1914

had almost doubled between 1820 and 1830, and Manchester's population had risen by 47 per cent. Transport of the necessities for both was checked by the monopolistic Bridgewater Canal; a large-scale competitor was necessary. Its demands almost exceeded the technology available: only on the eve of its completion, and under pressure of an open competition, was an efficient enough locomotive produced by the Stephensons. The difference between the award-winning *Rocket* (1830) and the production-line *Patentee* (1834), however, was almost as great as that between the *Rocket* and its clumsy if reliable precursor, the *Locomotion*. Locomotive design did not subsequently change for half a century.

In the 1830s, railway development was buoyed up by another speculative boom. By 1840 nearly 2,400 miles of track connected London with Birmingham, Manchester, and Brighton. Some of the new lines were prosperous; others, over-capitalized and faced with penal land and legal charges, ran into trouble. There were few enough rules in the early days of joint-stock companies, and the reputation soared of those who succeeded in turning 'scrip into gold', such as George Hudson, 'the Railway King', who controlled a third of the system by 1845. Hudson made his attractive profits by paying the dividends of existing lines with capital raised for new branches; when the great mania of the 1840s, which he helped promote, faltered in 1848, he was exposed and fled the country – but not before mileage had risen to over 8,000, and the network had been extended from Aberdeen to Plymouth.

Railway Heroes

But the railway age produced its heroes as well: the self-taught Stephenson and his brilliant son Robert, Joseph Locke, Daniel Gooch, and the polymath Isambard Kingdom Brunel, whose vast projects – the seven-foot-gauge Great Western Railway, the pioneer iron-and-screw steamer *Great Britain*, and the 18,000 ton sea-leviathan *Great Eastern* –

6. British engineers of the railway age, a posed group by John Lucas, ostensibly set in autumn 1849 in a hut on the edge of the Menai Straits during the hoisting into position of the tubular wrought-iron spans of Robert Stephenson's Menai Bridge (in background) on the Crewe–Holyhead railway. Stephenson is seated centre, and Isamabard Kingdom Brunel on the far right. Joseph Locke (seated second from right) completed the triumvirate of great railway engineers. All three died in their mid-fifties, worn out by overwork, in 1859–60.

fascinated the public as much as they terrified his unfortunate financial backers. 'What poet-race', G. K. Chesterton would later ask, 'shot such cyclopean arches at the stars?' Such men – Carlyle called them 'captains of industry' – were more attractive entrepreneurs than the cotton-masters, and Samuel Smiles was subsequently to make them paragons of 'self-help'.

Construction and Cost

This new transport system had been created in less than a score of years, and without any modern construction techniques. The 'navvies' – of whom 250,000 were said to be at work in 1848, powered by beer and beef – created the huge earthworks which characterized early British railways. The image of the British working man in the 1830s had been of the pathetic factory slave or starving cotton-weaver. In the 1850s it was provided by the brawny labourers who ran up the Crystal Palace in six months, and who were shipped to the Crimea to make good – with railways and camps – the incompetence of the military. The railways had cost an unprecedented amount of money, however: by 1849 no less than £224.6 million had been invested. In 1849 total receipts remained low at only £11.4 million; although receipts rose by 1859 to £24.4 million, railways were never more than a modest and reliable investment, and in the case of some companies they were far from that. Until 1852, they made more money from passengers than freight, and the subsequent expansion of goods traffic was obtained to a great extent by a systematic process of buying over their chief competitors, the canals, whose owners, having hitherto enjoyed inflated profits, were little inclined to see themselves beggared by competition. By the mid-1850s, strategic sections of the canal network were in railway ownership, and traffics were ruthlessly transferred to rail. Already, in the most dynamic area of industrial growth, the conspiracy of capitalists denounced by Adam Smith had become a fact.

Chapter 9
Politics and Diplomacy: Palmerston's Years

The railway boom coincided with a dramatic shift in politics. The harvests of 1842, 1843, and 1844 had been good; grain was plentiful and costs low. Then in 1845 the harvest was wrecked by bad weather, and the first blights hit the Irish potato crop. The arguments of the Anti-Corn Law League seemed confirmed. Peel attempted to carry free trade in Cabinet, failed, and resigned, only to come back when the Whigs could not form a ministry. In February 1846, he moved a package of measures abolishing duties on imported corn over three years. He thus bought – or hoped to buy – the support of the gentry through grants towards the Poor Law and local police forces. But his party was deeply split and only a minority supported him when he was censured on Irish coercion in May. In the ensuing election Russell came back with a Whig ministry, and Whigs and later Liberals dominated politics thereafter. Badly weakened by the shift of the Peelite elite, which included Gladstone, the earl of Aberdeen, and Sir James Graham, into the ambit of the Whigs, the Tory gentry now found themselves led by the ex-Whigs Lord Derby and Lord George Bentinck, and the exotic ex-radical Benjamin Disraeli. The Tories stood firm as a party, but held power for only 5 of the next 30 years.

Party Management, Landed Power

There was a greater degree of party management, centred on the new clubs of St James's, the Reform and the (Tory) Carlton, both founded in 1832, but to conceive of politics shading from left to right means imposing the criteria of a later age. National party organizations were as unknown as party programmes. Public speeches were rare. Leaders – still predominantly Whig magnates – would drop a few hints to their closest colleagues, often their relatives, about policy just before elections (which took place every seven years). Prospective candidates travelled to likely seats, issued addresses, and canvassed for the support of local notables, only 'going to the poll' if promised respectable support.

Huge expenses made contested elections the exception rather than the rule. The territorial nobility were impregnable in their many surviving 'pocket boroughs'. A vote – delivered in public – against, say, Blenheim Palace at Woodstock was still an almost suicidal move for a local farmer or tradesman. Counties, likewise, were dominated by the great families. The medium-sized boroughs were more open but expensive; their electors sometimes reached the levels of corruption depicted at Eatanswill in Charles Dickens's *Pickwick Papers*. The newly enfranchised great towns could sometimes elect active if impecunious men – Macaulay sat for Leeds – but more often favoured affluent local businessmen, who usually bore most of the cost of the contest. Some things, however, remain familiar today: England was more conservative, the 'Celtic fringe' more radical.

Although Wellington's brief caretaker ministry of 1834 proved the last occasion on which a duke became first minister, power lay with the landed interest, in which the Whigs were still as well represented as the Tories, although in many cases the elevation to this status was recent, a tribute to the flexibility of the elite. Peel and Gladstone – both Oxford double-firsts – were only a generation removed from provincial industry and commerce, and even more remarkable was the rise of Benjamin Disraeli, adventurer and novelist, stemming from a religion, Judaism, whose members were only to obtain full civil equality in 1860.

The Services

Ministries spent little time over domestic legislation, but much more over foreign and service affairs – not surprisingly, since the latter claimed more than a third of the estimates. Neither navy nor army had changed much since 1815. The navy bought its first steamer, a tug called the *Monkey*, in 1822. With enormous reluctance, others were ordered in 1828, the Lords of the Admiralty feeling that 'the introduction of steam is calculated to strike a fatal blow at the supremacy of the Empire'. Paddles meant a loss of broadside guns, and sailing ships could keep station for years, so Devonport was still launching all-sail three-deckers in 1848, although the successful use of screw propulsion on smaller ships was numbering the days of the sailing fleet. The old long-service army of about 130,000 men – 42 per cent Irish and 14 per cent Scots in 1830 – poorly paid and wretchedly accommodated, kept the peace in Ireland and the colonies. In many small campaigns it advanced Britain's spheres of influence and trade in India, and in the 'Opium War' of 1839–42 in China, although now on behalf of free-trading merchants rather than the fading Chartered Companies.

Withdrawal from Europe

Britain's withdrawal from European commitments was reflected, too, in diplomacy. After the defeat of Napoleon, the Continental conservative leaders, above all Tsar Alexander I of Russia, tried to establish a system of co-operation in Europe through regular congresses of the great powers. But even in 1814 British diplomats preferred security to be achieved by the traditional means of the balance of power, even if this meant resurrecting France as a counterweight to Russia. For much of the time between then and 1848, a tacit Anglo-French *entente* subsisted, though it was disturbed in 1830 when Catholic Belgium detached itself from Holland, and looked as if it might fall into the French sphere of influence. The solution to this was found in Belgian neutrality, and a new royal family with close links with Britain – all guaranteed by the Treaty of London (1839), whose violation by Germany in August 1914 brought the long peace to an end.

Other problems between Britain and France were less easily settled, as they were linked with the steady decline of the Turkish Empire, which Britain wished to maintain as a buffer against Austria and Russia in the Balkans. For much of this period, the dominant figure was Viscount Palmerston, who, coming late into foreign affairs in 1830 at the age of 46, burrowed himself into the grubby premises of the Foreign Office in Whitehall (which at the zenith of its power had a staff of only 45) and stayed there as the dominant force for over 30 years – aggressively patriotic, but still, within limits, liberal. In 1847, however, the most celebrated British politician in Europe was not Palmerston but Richard Cobden, the apostle of free trade. He was feted in capital after capital, and his hosts were sure of one thing – the conservative monarchies were doomed, and the day of liberalism would shortly dawn.

The Year of Revolutions

Early in 1848, Marx and Engels drafted the *Communist Manifesto* in London, prophesying, on behalf of a small group of German socialists, a European revolution, to be led by the workers of those countries most advanced towards capitalism. Paris rose up against Louis Philippe on 24 February, then Berlin, Vienna, and the Italian states erupted. But Britain did not follow. There was a momentary panic when the Chartists brought their last great petition to London on 14 April; 10,000 special constables were sworn in; the telegraphs bought over for the week by the Home Office to stop the Chartists using them. The constables were potentially more worrying than the Chartists, as middle-class volunteer forces had spearheaded the Continental risings. But their loyalty was absolute; revolutions were something that happened elsewhere. The Chartists dispersed from Kennington Common; Parliament laughed the great petition out.

But there was no repetition of 1793 either. The republican government in Paris wanted to maintain co-operation with Britain, acted firmly against its own radicals, and did not try to export revolution. Palmerston wanted no change in the balance of power, but favoured constitutional regimes and an Austrian withdrawal from Italy. This moderation was scarcely successful, and Britain was unable to guarantee any of the gains that the liberals briefly made. A combination of peasant support bought by land reform and Russian aid, which crushed Hungary and gave Austria a free hand elsewhere, brought the *anciens régimes* back to power – but Austria was now prostrate and the Russians worryingly dominant in Eastern Europe.

Chapter 10
Incorporation

Repeal of the Corn Law, the handling of the 1848 emergency, and the rapid expansion of the railways not only made the economic situation more hopeful but underpinned it with a new political consensus. The agricultural interest had been checked, but its farming efficiency enabled it to ride out foreign competition. At the same time the bourgeoisie realized that it had both to co-operate with the old elite in controlling the industrial workers, and to concede enough to the latter to stave off political explosions. In this context (particularly compared with textiles), railways, steamers, and telegraphs were all useful and glamorous – attractive advertisements for industrialization. Functionally, they brought together land, commerce, and industry. And they made lawyers in particular very rich.

Gradual Reform

By the 1850s the law 'incorporated' the working classes – or, at least, their leading members. The 'New Model' trade unions of skilled workers, such as the Engineers and the Carpenters, pressed not for drastic state intervention but for contractual equality. They acted not through public demonstrations but through diplomatic pressure on MPs of both parties. Their procedures and iconography rejected the oaths and mysticism of the old quasi-conspiratorial societies for an almost pedantic legalism, concerned with defending their respectability at the top of the working class.

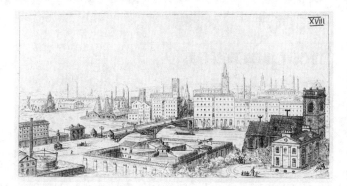

7. An industrialized town depicted in *Contrasts* (1840), by A. W. N. Pugin, in which the great Gothic revival architect attacked classical architecture, religious heterodoxy (the places of worship of no fewer than nine denominations are shown), and the heartlessness of industrial society with its grim, machine-like buildings. The gaol in front is a version of Jeremy Bentham's 'Panopticon'

Economic and social theory moved towards the idea of 'incorporation'. Classical economics had earlier been subversive and pessimistic: one strand of it, in the hands of Marx, remained so. But John Stuart Mill in his *Logic* of 1840 and his *Political Economy* of 1848 reconciled utilitarianism with gradual reform and sympathy for the aims of moderate working-class leaders. Mill found to his surprise that the *Logic*, with its substantial borrowings from the French sociological tradition of Henri de Saint-Simon and Auguste Comte, became the orthodoxy of the older universities, which were recuperating from the traumas of the Oxford Movement. But the 'Saint of Rationalism' himself had, in his enthusiasm for the English Romantic poets, gone far to make his blend of utilitarianism, ethical individualism, and reformist 'socialism' acceptable to reformers within the establishment, who broadcast it in the high-minded literary reviews which burgeoned around the mid-century.

In the eyes of the candidates for political incorporation, 'the rule of law' was far from absolute. A. V. Dicey, who applied the phrase to nineteenth-century government, was himself to write in the 1860s: 'John Smith *qua* John Smith cannot be suppressed, but John Smith *qua* artisan can.' But he expected that the extension of the franchise would end such inequities – as, by and large, it did.

'Without the Law'

Who then remained 'without the law'? The Irish had been wounded too deeply. 'Repeal of the Union' was O'Connell's bequest to a new generation of patriots. Although the Catholic middle class, like the Scots, proved anxious to find niches in the British establishment, Irish nationalists were made more aggressive by the famine, and could in the future count on the aid of their embittered emigrant brethren in America. Settlers in the colonies may have prided themselves on their transplanting of British institutions, but as the Colonial Office was aware, settler notions of law found no place for the rights of the natives. High and low churchmen complained when the courts upheld the vague and all-embracing formulas of the Broad Church establishment. They could not dislodge it but they could indelibly affect the skyline of Victorian cities and the practice of piety.

The intellectuals accepted the notion of political and social evolution – Tennyson's 'freedom slowly broadens down / from precedent to precedent' – long before Darwin's *Origin of Species* appeared in 1859. Although no friend to liberalism, Carlyle's commendations of self-reliance and the work ethic gave individualism an almost religious quality. John Stuart Mill became a pillar of the mid-Victorian Liberal Party, eccentric only in his desire to extend 'incorporation' to the half of the population whom politics ignored – women (whose slow progress to civic and legal equality started, however, to accelerate during the 1850s). Two more troubled intellects were difficult to pin down. John Ruskin, 'the graduate of Oxford' whose *Modern Painters* was the sensation of 1843, combined reverence for aristocracy with increasingly subversive views on the economy and the environment; though his directly political impact was to be minimal compared to that of Owen. No one savaged the law's delays and inequities more energetically than Dickens, yet no one worried more about the results of revolution and lawlessness. The Circumlocution Office, the Tite Barnacles, Jarndyce versus Jarndyce, were balanced by Slackbridge, Madame Defarge, and Bill Sikes, though Dicey got it just about right when, on balance, he put Dickens alongside Shaftesbury as a force pushing public opinion towards 'positive' reforming legislation.

Novels and Ballads

Nineteenth-Century Britain

Militant dissent and old radicalism had their own world-view, remote from that of the establishment, but its tentacles reached out towards them. The middle class read 'industrial novels,' such as Disraeli's *Sybil*, in the 1840s, anxious about and intrigued by conditions in the great towns, trying to personalize their problems and reconcile them with individualist morality. But Mrs Gaskell in *Mary Barton* and Kingsley in *Alton Locke* could not provide any such assurance; the only effective solution for their most heroic characters was emigration. Dickens's savage Carlylean satire on Manchester, *Hard Times*, wavered and collapsed when it came to considering any better future for the inhabitants of Coketown.

But few of the Coketown people had time or money to read about what the literati thought of their plight, and little enough was known about what they read, although it was obviously affected by the co-option of the literary radicals by a middle-class public. Mayhew, the social investigator of the *Morning Chronicle*, just about carried on the journalistic tradition of Cobbett and William Hazlitt into the 1860s; Dickens, from the same Bohemian milieu, shifted away from it. We know that the 'labour aristocracy' in the trade unions read what their betters wanted them to read; that the religious kept their Bibles and their *Pilgrim's Progress*; but what of the 'roughs', and 'tavern society'? A folk tradition survived and developed in the fishing ports, among the weavers, and on the farms. Later in the nineteenth century, an American professor discovered two-thirds of the great traditional English ballads still being sung in the 'Farmtouns' of north-east Scotland, where the more plebeian 'bothy ballads' acted as a means of spreading information about farmers among the ploughmen and carters, and the 'Society of the Horseman's Word' conserved a primitive, but effective, trade unionism.

In his novel *Except the Lord* (1953) about the mid-Victorian youth of a radical politician, Joyce Cary takes his hero, Chester Nimmo, into a fairground tent. A troupe of actors are performing *Maria Marten, or the Murder in the Red Barn*, a staple of nineteenth-century melodrama, loosely based on an actual murder which occurred in 1830 – the eve of 'Captain Swing'. This was Nimmo's reaction:

> The drama that we saw, and that millions had seen, was a story of the cruellest hurt of many inflicted by the rich on the poor. Throughout the play everything possible was done to show the virtue, innocence and helplessness of the poor, and the abandoned cruelty, the heartless self-indulgence of the rich.
>
> And this was one among hundreds of such plays. I have wondered often how such propaganda failed to bring to England also, as to France, Italy, Germany, almost every other nation, a bloody revolution, for its power was incredible. As I say, it was decisive in my own life . . .

Cary, a subtle and historically aware novelist, seems to have sensed here a resentment and grievance deep enough to be concealed by the respectability and self-help of formal working-class politics but for which political 'incorporation', the repetitive rows of sanitarily adequate workmen's dwellings, the increasingly opulent chapels, the still-locked Sunday parks, offered no consolation.

Chapter 11

Free Trade: An Industrial Economy Rampant

The Great Exhibition of 1851 celebrated the ascendancy of the United Kingdom in the market-place of the world, though many of the Continental exhibits, especially those from the German states, gave British manufacturers pause when the high quality of their technology was examined. The Exhibition, sponsored by the court and organized by the aristocracy, reflected Britain's commitment to economic progress and hence to Liberalism. It touched an enthusiastic nerve in the popular mind. For many ordinary people, it was the first occasion for a visit to London, an exhausting but exhilarating long day-trip on one of the special trains which brought visitors from all over the country. The success of the Exhibition astonished contemporaries. Figures for attendance were published daily in the press; by the end, over six million tickets had been sold, and on one day over 100,000 persons visited the 'blazing arch of lucid glass', Joseph Paxton's Crystal Palace which housed the Exhibition in Hyde Park. Its substantial profits were later used to build the museums at South Kensington.

The huge crowds were well behaved and openly monarchic. Members of the propertied classes congratulated themselves: the nervous, brittle atmosphere of the 1840s was giving way to the calmer tone of the 1850s, which by the 1860s had become positively self-confident. A street ballad sold at the Exhibition emphasized the curious blend of artisan self-reliance, free-trade internationalism, and monarchic chauvinism which was to define the language of much of British public life for the rest of the century:

> O, surely England's greatest wealth,
> Is an honest working man. . . .
> It is a glorious sight to see
> So many thousands meet,
> Not heeding creed or country,
> Each other friendly greet.
> Like children of one mighty sire,
> May that sacred tie ne'er cease,
> May the blood stain'd sword of War give way
> To the Olive branch of Peace.
>
> But hark! the trumpets flourish,
> Victoria does approach,
> That she may long be spared to us
> Shall be our reigning toast.
> I trust each heart, it will respond,
> To what I now propose –
> Good will and plenty to her friends,
> And confusion to her foes.

The tone of ballads such as this explains the popularity of Henry Temple, Lord Palmerston. When Lord Aberdeen's coalition government of 1852 foundered into war against Russia in the Crimea (1854–6) and then disintegrated when the ineptitude of the war effort was revealed, Palmerston emerged from its ruins as prime minister. He held this post, leading the Liberal coalition, with one short interruption, until his death in October 1865. Palmerston personified the bombastic self-confidence of Britain as the only world power, and succeeded in being simultaneously an aristocrat, a reformer, a free-trader, an internationalist, and a chauvinist.

The 1851 Consensus

The society which the Great Exhibition of 1851 revealed was given more statistical analysis in the Census of the same year. Two facts captured the public imagination. For the first time, more people in the mainland of the United Kingdom lived in towns – albeit often quite small ones – than in the countryside: a dramatic contrast with the past and with any other economy. The free-trade movement accompanied rather than anticipated the commitment of the British economy to manufacturing, transport, and service industries with an urban base. That dream of the Liberal Tories of the 1820s, that the economy could be somehow held in balance between agriculture and industry, was forgotten with the free-trade dawn. Agriculture remained easily the largest single industry and indeed increased its competence and output markedly in the 1850s and 1860s. But the growth of population was in the towns, and labourers left the land for the cities.

When agriculture faced its crisis in the 1870s with the opening of the North American prairies, there were relatively few left to defend it. The 'Revolt of the Field' in the 1870s was a motley affair, as out-of-work labourers struggled to organize themselves as wages fell and magistrates and farmers brought in the troops to harvest the crops. By the 1850s, Britain – and especially northern and midland England, south Wales, and southern Scotland – was thus, through the working of Adam Smith's 'invisible hand' of world trade rather than by any conscious political decision, committed to a ride on the roller-coaster of international capitalism, a ride where the travellers could not see beyond the rise or dip ahead of them: no one had been there before. An urban nation had no precedent. Perhaps that was why the British dwelt so tenaciously on rural images and traditions.

The other statistic of the 1851 Census that caught the attention of contemporaries was its revelations about religion. It was the only Census ever to attempt to assess English religious attendance, or the lack of it. There were difficulties about the statistics, but the main emphasis was indisputable and surprising: England and Wales were only partly church-going, and Anglicans were in only a bare majority of those who attended. Of a total population of 17,927,609, the church-goers were:

Church of England	5,292,551
Roman Catholics	383,630
Protestant Dissenters	4,536,265

Of potential church-goers, over 5.25 million stayed at home. The Census was a triumph for non-Anglicans. Their claim to greater political representation and attention was now backed by that most potent of all mid-Victorian weapons, so approved of by Mr Gradgrind, Dickens's Lancastrian manufacturer: 'a fact'.

England in the 1850s was thus increasingly urban, perhaps increasingly secular, certainly increasingly non-Anglican in tone. Mid-Victorian politics reflected these tendencies, all of which pointed towards Liberalism.

Liberalism

Between 1847 and 1868, the Tories (the rump of the party left as protectionists after the 1846 split) lost six general elections running (1847, 1852, 1857, 1859, 1865, 1868). It is clear that the Tories lost these elections; it is less easy to say who won them. Majority governments relied on support from four main groups: the Whigs, the radicals, the Liberals, and the Peelites (the followers of Peel in 1846). This support was always liable to disintegration. The classic mid-Victorian political pattern was as follows: a coalition government was made up of all or most of the above groups, compromising and bargaining until they could agree no more and a point of breakdown was reached: the government would go out of office without dissolving Parliament; the

Tories would then form a minority government, during which the non-Tory groups would resolve their differences, defeat the Tories, force a dissolution, win the general election, and resume power. This overall pattern explains the minority Tory (Derby/Disraeli) ministries of 1852, 1858–9, and 1866–8.

The political system between 1846 and 1868 thus excluded the Tories from power, while allowing them occasional periods of minority office. During the same period, the majority coalition first formed by Lord Aberdeen in 1852 gradually fused itself into 'the liberal party', though even when it became regularly referred to by that name in the 1860s it remained fissiparous and liable to disintegration. At the executive level, the Whigs, the Peelites, and Lord Palmerston predominated. To a considerable extent they ruled on sufferance. That great surge of middle-class political awareness exemplified in the Anti-Corn Law League in the 1840s had made it clear to politicians that the old political structure could be maintained only if it came to terms with middle-class expectations. The series of great budgets introduced by the Peelite chancellor of the Exchequer, Gladstone, in the years 1853–5 and 1859–65 went far towards meeting these expectations fiscally. The manufacturing classes wanted free trade: Gladstone saw that they got it.

'Free Trade'

'Free trade' of course meant much more than simply the abolition of protective tariffs. 'Free trade' or *laissez-faire* were shorthand terms exemplifying a whole philosophy of political, social, and economic organization. John Stuart Mill's 1848 *Principles of Political Economy*, the handbook of mid-Victorian liberalism, put the point in a nutshell: 'Laisser-faire, in short, should be the general practice: every departure from it, unless required by some great good, is a certain evil.' The presumption was that the State should stand aside. The division which Mill and others made between 'the State' on the one hand and society on the other was based on the assumption that the individual could and should stand alone. Individualism, self-respect, self-reliance, and the organization of voluntary and co-operative societies were the keynotes of mid-Victorian liberalism. Thus the economy should be self-regulating, and individuals, whether consumers or producers, holding their copies of Samuel Smiles's *Self-Help* (1859), should be free to make what way they could in it.

This view of individualism gained from the widely popular writings of the social evolutionists. Charles Darwin's *On the Origin of Species* (1859) was not a bolt from the blue: it fitted naturally into, as well as transcending, a corpus of writing on evolution. The concept of evolution, and consequently of 'progress', whether on the individual, national, or global level, came to permeate every aspect of Victorian life and thought. Because evolution was determined by laws of science (a view usually described as 'positivism'), man's duty was to discover and obey such laws, not meddle with them. Hence most positivists (such as Walter Bagehot, editor of the influential weekly *Economist*, and Herbert Spencer, author of many works on sociology) were strong *laissez-faire* supporters.

Knowledge Untaxed

If individuals were to make their way productively, they must be prepared and equipped with knowledge: the availability of knowledge and the freedom to comment on it was thus central to a liberal society. Moral choices must be informed choices: self-awareness and self-development in the context of human sympathy were the themes of the novels of George Eliot (Mary Ann Evans), and her own life was a testimony to the trials as well as the liberation of the free spirit in mid-Victorian society.

The abolition in 1855 and 1861 of the 'Taxes on Knowledge' (the stamp duties on newspapers, and the customs and excise duties on paper) epitomized the sort of liberal legislation which was particularly prized. The repeal of these taxes made possible the phenomenon which was both the epitome and the guarantor of liberal Britain – the liberal metropolitan and provincial press. The 1850s and 1860s saw a spectacular expansion of daily and Sunday newspapers, especially in the provinces, overwhelmingly liberal in politics and in general outlook. By 1863, there were over 1,000 newspapers in Britain, the vast majority of very recent foundation. For example, in Yorkshire in 1867, 66 of the 86 local newspapers had been founded since 1853. In London, the *Daily Telegraph*, refounded in 1855 as a penny daily and as the flagship of the liberal press, had a circulation of almost 200,000 in 1871, far outstripping *The Times*. The new provincial press took its tone from the *Telegraph*, and that tone was unabashedly and enthusiastically progressive. A typical example is this leader commenting on Gladstone's tour of the Newcastle shipyards in 1862:

> When we pull a political pansy for Lord Derby [the Tory leader], and tell him 'that's for remembrance', it is because the violent fallacies and frenzies of Protection are not to be forgotten simply because they are forgiven ... With ten years' honour upon her green laurels, and the French treaty [of free trade signed in 1860] in her hand – the emblem of future conquests – we have enshrined Free Trade at last in a permanent seat.

Fiscal policy

By the 1860s, free trade – in its specific sense of an absence of protective tariffs – had become a central orthodoxy of British politics, almost as entrenched as the Protestant succession. The triumph of the classical political economists was complete, in that the cardinal tenet of their faith was established as a political principle so widely accepted that only a deliberately perverse or self-confessedly unreconstructed politician would deny it. Front-bench Tory politicians quickly took the view that if their party was again to become a majority party, they must accept that protection was 'not only dead but damned', as Disraeli said. Tory budgets became as impeccably free-trading as Liberal ones.

The Churches

Outside the area of fiscal policy, there was less agreement about how far 'free trade' should go. Pressure groups within the Liberal movement in the 1850s and 1860s promoted a large range of 'negative' free-trade measures: the abolition of established Churches, the abolition of compulsory church rates, the abolition of religious tests for entry into Oxford and Cambridge and public offices, the removal of restrictions upon the transfer or use of land, the end of a civil service based on patronage. In addition to these, there was in the 1860s a general movement in the constituencies for further parliamentary reform – a demand welcomed by many but not all of the Liberal MPs.

The Liberal Party legislating on such matters was not really a 'party' in the modern sense of the word. It was rather a loose coalition of complex, interlocking allegiances, the most basic of which was its commitment to a free-trading economy. Within the coalition nestled many reforming interests, especially of a religious sort. A great religious revival in the 1860s added to the number of religious activists within the Liberal Party, and to the enthusiasm with which they both aired their opinions and worked for the party's success. Roman Catholics, nonconformists, and even secularists found voices within this broadly based movement for progress – the voices were given a common accent by their hostility to Anglicanism and the established Church. Non-Anglicanism was, throughout the century, perhaps the most important social reason for voting Liberal.

Paradoxically, however, the leadership of the coalition was uniformly Anglican, though of a moderate and reforming kind. There was, therefore, considerable dispute between the leadership of the coalition and its more militant supporters about the speed of reform. On the whole, the leadership – Palmerston, Lord John Russell, Gladstone – wanted moderate reform which would strengthen the Anglican Church overall, while the radical rank and file wanted step-by-step reform which would lead to the eventual disestablishment of the Anglican Church. Both groups could thus agree on limited measures such as the abolition of compulsory church rates while disagreeing on the ultimate ends of their policies. The crowning success of this sort of approach to politics was the disestablishment of the Anglican Church in Ireland in 1869.

Franchise Reform

The participation of the articulate members of the working classes within the Liberal Party, especially at the constituency level, was of great importance. In the 1830s and early 1840s, the six points of the Chartists had constituted a demand which, in terms of the politics of the day, could not be incorporated by the classes holding political power. By the late 1850s, radical movement for constitutional reform, often led by ex-Chartists, demanded only changes in the franchise, and of these enfranchisement of the male head of each household at most ('household suffrage'). It was not difficult for political leaders in both parties, but especially in the Liberal Party, to come to terms with such requests.

They also had their own reasons for wanting to change the system. Some Tories wanted to change it because their experience from 1847 onwards showed that they could not win a general election within the existing system. Some Liberals, including Gladstone and Lord John Russell, wanted to make marginal extensions to the franchise so as to include more liberal artisans, sturdy individualists who would support the Liberals' programme of retrenchment and reform. Some radicals, such as John Bright, wanted a 'household suffrage' to give a more full-blooded basis to Liberalism, though even they were quick to point out that they did not want votes given to what was known as 'the residuum' (that is, paupers, the unemployed, the 'thriftless', men with no property at all). Some Liberals, such as Robert Lowe, radical enough on ordinary legislation, distrusted any change leading to 'democracy', as they believed the 'intelligent class' would be swamped by it. Some Tories such as the future Lord Salisbury feared a household suffrage would lead to an attack on property through increased direct taxes such as the income tax. Some Whigs saw no reason to change a system which always returned non-Tory Parliaments.

Palmerston reflected the views of this last group, and won a great election victory in 1865 without a pledge to franchise reform. He died that autumn. Russell, his successor as prime minister, brought in with Gladstone in 1866 a very moderate reform bill dealing mainly with towns, on which their ministry broke up, some of their party withdrawing support because the bill did too much, others because it did too little. The third of the Derby/Disraeli minority Tory administrations then brought in its own bill for the towns, thus selling the pass of the anti-reformers' position.

Reform of some sort became certain: the Liberals had begun their customary regrouping when Disraeli unexpectedly announced his acceptance of a household suffrage amendment: the bill then passed, in a form a great deal more dramatic and sweeping than the Russell–Gladstone bill of the previous year. The franchise system of 1832 was ended: the parameters of urban politics until 1915 were established (similar voting privileges were granted to men in the counties in 1884–5). In an extremely confused situation in 1868, the Liberals seemed to reconfirm their 1865 election position as the dominant party by winning the general election with the huge majority of 112.

In fact, the 1867 Reform Act had changed the rules of the political game in such a way that a majority Tory government again became possible – but it was to be a Tory government under Disraeli in 1874, which made no serious attempt to reverse any of the main Liberal achievements of the previous 30 years, certainly not the centrepiece of free trade.

Gladstone's First Government

The early years of Gladstone's first government (1868–74) were the culmination of these reforming pressures: by 1874 many of the demands of mid-century Liberalism were fulfilled. In addition to disestablishing the Irish Church, the Liberals in the 1860s and early 1870s had abolished compulsory church rates, the 'taxes on knowledge', religious tests for Oxford and Cambridge, and the purchase of commissions in the army; they had legislated on Irish land, and on education for England and Scotland; they had opened the civil service to entrance by competition; and they had made capitalism relatively safe for the investor by introducing limited liability – all this in addition to their preoccupation with free-trade finance, proper government accounting, minimum budgets, and retrenchment.

Though there was the usual tug and tussle of political bargaining, this great reforming surge had not been seriously opposed. Even the establishment of the Anglican Church – whose defence in toto had been a central rallying point of Toryism in the first half of the century – had been ended in part clearly and efficiently: what had in the 1830s been merely a radical dream had by the 1870s become reality, and almost without apparent struggle. The Tories' ultimate card, the unelected House of Lords, had been played in only a limited way – to delay repeal of the paper duties, to delay church rate repeal, the ballot, and the abolition of religious tests at the universities. The propertied and labouring classes had collaborated in a great clearing of the decks of the Liberal ship of State.

Economic Boom

The advent of 'free trade' as the prevailing ethos coincided with an economic boom, lasting from the early 1850s to the early 1870s. Contemporaries saw the first as causing the second; economic historians have been more sceptical. The removal of tariff barriers

8. The Forth Bridge under construction, 1888-9, completing the railway network, which reached its zenith in the 1890s

probably had only a marginal impact on the British economy, but the ascendancy of 'free trade', in its larger sense of a national commitment to economic progress, was closely related to an entrepreneurial enthusiasm which all classes seem to have shared.

The mid-century boom was not, in percentage terms, very spectacular, and it was linked to a mild inflation. But it was nonetheless extremely important, for it seemed to show that the 'condition of England' question which had been so much a preoccupation of the 1820–50 period could be solved – was being solved – by market forces working within the existing social and political structure. Even the distress caused by the 'cotton famine' of the 1860s in Lancashire – when the cotton mills were cut off by the American Civil War from their traditional source of raw material, the plantations in the Southern States – produced little prolonged political reaction, and the propertied classes congratulated themselves that local initiative and voluntary subscriptions had seemed to be sufficient to allow the Westminster government to avoid accepting any direct responsibility for the sufferings of the Lancastrian work-force (though in fact a government loan scheme had also been important).

Compared with any other country, the British economy in the period 1850–70 was extraordinary in its complexity and in the range of its products and activities. It was strong in the basic raw materials of an early industrial economy – coal and iron – and it increased its world ascendancy in these two commodities as Continental countries imported British coal and iron to supply the basic materials for their own industrialization. An energetic manufacturing sector pressed forward with a huge range of items, from ships and steam engines through textiles to the enormous variety of small manufactured goods which adorned Victorian houses and, by their export in British ships, 'Victorianized' the whole trading world. This intense industrial activity rested on a sound currency and on a banking system which, though it had its failures, was comparatively stable and was, especially from the 1870s, gaining an increasingly important role in the economy.

Chapter 12
A Shifting Population: Town and Country

This surge of economic progress produced a nation and an economy whose preoccupations were by 1870 largely industrial and urban. The growth of towns, which some had thought in 1851 could hardly be continued, intensified. By 1901, only one-fifth of the population of England and Wales lived in what may be called 'rural areas'; that is, 80 per cent of the population was urbanized, a far greater proportion than in any European country, and one which remained little changed until the 1970s. By 1901, there were 74 towns with over 50,000 inhabitants and London – 'the metropolis' as Victorians called it – grew from 2.3 million in 1851 to 4.5 million in 1911 (or 7.3 million if we include all its suburbs).

The most rapid growth was not in the already established 'industrial revolution' cities, such as Liverpool and Manchester, but in the clusters of towns around the industrial heartland, towns such as Salford. These areas of urban sprawl went to make up what Patrick Geddes, the late-Victorian theorist of town planning, called 'conurbations'; that is, large areas of industrial and urban land in which several cities merge to form what is really a single non-rural unit. By 1911, Britain had seven such areas, at a time when no European country had more than two. These were: Greater London (7.3 million), south-east Lancashire (2.1 million), the West Midlands (1.6 million), West Yorkshire (1.5 million), Merseyside (1.2 million), Tyneside (0.8 million), and central Clydeside (about 1.5

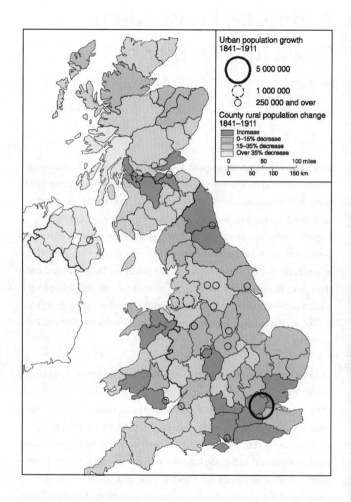

Map 3. Urban population growth, 1841–1911

million) – all this in a nation with a population of only 40 million on the mainland in 1911. Some towns, such as the iron and steel town of Middlesbrough, grew from virtually nothing to a population of 120,000 in half a century. Most of these conurbations contained a significant Irish community, and their politics consequently tended to be more 'orange and green' than elsewhere. At the end of the century London and Leeds also absorbed large Jewish communities, the victims of an Eastern European 'rural depopulation' as ferocious as the Irish Famine.

Urban Conditions

Urban growth at this sort of pace was, of course, to be a common phenomenon in underdeveloped countries in the twentieth century, but in the nineteenth it had no precedent. It is not easy to generalize about these towns. Styles and standards of architecture varied enormously, from the indestructible stone tenements of Glasgow, through the 'back-to-backs' of Yorkshire and 'two-up, two-down' little houses in the mining towns, often built of poor-quality brick, to the decorous suburbs of the lower and upper middle classes. A common feature of this housing was that it was almost all leased or rented – owner-occupiers were rare, though becoming more common by the end of the century. Some towns were well planned by civic-minded local councils, with parks, libraries, concert halls, and baths; others were left to the mercy of the speculative builder.

These growing towns were dominated by the railways, which created for the first time a nationally integrated economy. They transformed the centres of towns by the space which their stations and marshalling yards took up, they made it possible for better-off people to live away from the town centre by providing cheap transport from the suburbs, and they covered everything with soot. Filth and noise characterized Victorian cities – filth from the trains, the chimneys of factories and houses, and the horses, noise from the carts and carriages and horses on the cobblestones. When motor transport began to replace horses in

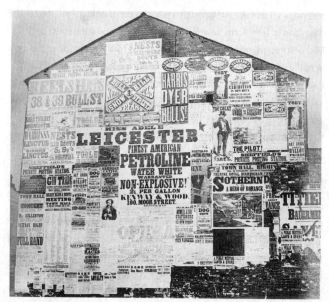

9. Victorian eclecticism: Birmingham advertisements at the time of the 1868 general election

the early twentieth century, everyone noticed how relatively quiet and clean town centres became.

But noise, filth, and bad housing are relative to what people are accustomed to: it was only slowly that the demand for improvement in urban life became a powerful one. For many Victorians, production was its own justification. This view was well expressed by Florence, Lady Bell, in her book *At the Works*, a classic study of a classic industrial town, Middlesbrough, given over to one pursuit and one only – the making of iron:

> In default of a romantic past, of a stately tradition, the fact of this swift gigantic growth has given to Middlesbrough a romance and dignity of

another kind, the dignity of power, of being able to stand erect by its sheer strength on no historical foundation, unsupported by the pedestals of Time ... And although it may not have the charm and beauty of antiquity, no manufacturing town ... can fail to have an interest and picturesqueness all its own ... Tall chimneys, great uncouth shapes of kilns and furnaces that appear through the smoke of a winter afternoon like turrets and pinnacles ... Twilight and night are the conditions under which to see an ironmaking town, the pillars of cloud by day, the pillars of fire by night.

The dynamism of the towns was, in the 20 years after the Great Exhibition, and partly inspired by the machinery exhibited at it, mirrored in the countryside. 'High farming' – capital spending on fertilizers, drainage, buildings, farm machinery such as reapers and threshers, roads linking with the new railways – apparently belied the argument that free trade spelt doom for the countryside, and led to considerable modernization, moral as well as physical. Even in the countryside there were fears for the continuance of traditional religion, as many turned to nonconformity and some to materialism.

Agricultural Depression

An energetic and aggressive farming generation won the profits which maintained the sedate, leisured, county society depicted in Trollope's novels of Barsetshire. In 1868, 80 per cent of food consumed in the United Kingdom was still home-produced. But despite 'high farming', many areas, especially in Ireland and Scotland, remained woefully under-capitalized, the foot-plough and hand-winnowing still being common in the north and west Highlands in the early twentieth century.

In the 1870s, a series of bad harvests, the opening of the North American prairies, faster and cheaper shipping thence and from the overseas wool-producing areas led to 'the great depression'. Only milk,

10. The agricultural depression. Farm labourers evicted at Milbourne St Andrew, Dorset, in 1874, for belonging to Joseph Arch's National Agricultural Labourers Union

hay, and straw production were not open to harsh foreign competition. In particular, the price of grain, the characteristic product of the eastern side of the country, fell dramatically, but farmers, especially the smaller ones, were slow to accept the permanence of this fall, or to adapt to the new demand for dairy products. The pastoral west was less severely affected.

The significance of agriculture in the economy declined as towns grew, a decline made swifter by the depression: in 1851 agriculture accounted for 20.3 per cent of the national income, in 1901 only 6.4 per cent, and the majority of British food and agricultural raw materials such as wool were imported – a fact which was to be of considerable strategic importance. Cries for the protection of agriculture received little response, even within the Tory Party – certainly not to the point of an alteration to the fiscal system of free trade. Some Liberal land reformers – for whom protection was axiomatically ruled out – advocated smallholdings (the 'three acres and a cow' campaign of

1885) as a solution; the establishment of the Crofting Commission (1886) for the Scottish Highlands, empowered to establish crofting communities free from landlord interference, was the only substantial achievement on the mainland, though a notable one in its long-term results.

The attraction of higher wages for fewer hours in the towns, mechanization in the 1850s and 1860s, and depression in the last quarter of the century led to extensive rural depopulation – a great exodus mostly to the Scottish and English towns, some to the coalfields (especially in Wales), some to the colonies, some to the army. Between 1861 and 1901 the decrease in the total of rural male labourers in England and Wales was just over 40 per cent; the total of women, less easily employable in the towns, decreased less dramatically, leaving a marked imbalance of the sexes in the countryside, though many unmarried women found their way into domestic service in the towns aided by such agencies as the Girls' Friendly Society.

Rural Decay

All this left rural society demoralized and neglected, with the passivity characteristic of communities in decay. Thomas Hardy's novels, whose span of publication (1872–96) covered almost exactly the years of the agricultural depression, captured majestically the uncontrollable and distant forces which seemed to determine the fate of the country communities and their inhabitants. Hardy wrote of country habits and traditions which had passed away but, though historical in form, the novels had a contemporary overtone. *The Mayor of Casterbridge* described the fate of Michael Henchard, a corn merchant whose failure to adapt to new methods of trading brought him to ruin. Hardy observed of him at the moment of his financial crash: 'The movements of his mind seemed to tend to the thought that some power was working against him.' The 'general drama of pain' which the Wessex novels depict was the disintegration of a civilization. Surveying his novels as a whole in 1895, Hardy observed:

> The change at the root of this has been the recent supplanting of the class of stationary cottagers, who carried on the local traditions and humours, by a population of more or less migratory labourers, which has led to a break of continuity in local history, more fatal than any other thing to the preservation of legend, folk-lore, close intersocial relations, and eccentric individualities. For these the indispensable conditions of existence are attachment to the soil of one particular spot by generation after generation.

Fortunately, Cecil Sharp, Marjorie Kennedy-Fraser, and other folklore and folk-song and dance historians recorded something of the quality of British rural life before it was wholly lost.

The breaking up of country customs was encouraged by Whitehall and Westminster. Educational measures – for example, the 1872 Scottish Education Act – worked to Anglicize the Gaelic-speakers of Scotland and Ireland and the Welsh-speakers of Wales, and to equip the peasantry for urban life. Between 1850 and 1900 rural change and education policy dealt those languages a powerful and in Scotland almost a fatal blow. In Wales, however, local initative secured the teaching of Welsh in schools from 1889.

Urban–Rural Relations

In some areas, there was a good deal of movement between town and country, as migrant workers left the towns for the harvest, and poaching by the inhabitants of small towns in the surrounding countryside was common. Some industrial workers, especially coalminers, lived in villages with moors and fields at their doors, and their sports, such as whippet and pigeon racing, had rural associations. Middle-class people took advantage of low land values to buy up a country place. For the financially sharp members of the propertied classes, the countryside became an expensive playground, a place for 'week-ending'; but for many urban-dwellers in the great cities it became a remote, even dangerous, place populated by a curious people with antique accents, clothes, and manners. Oscar Wilde's comedy, *The Importance of Being Earnest* (1895) caught the metropolitan tone:

LADY BRACKNELL: . . . land has ceased to be either a profit or a pleasure. It gives one position, and prevents one from keeping it up. That's all that can be said about land.

JACK: I have a country house with some land, of course, attached to it, about fifteen hundred acres, I believe; but I don't depend on that for my real income. In fact, as far as I can make out, the poachers are the only people who make anything out of it.

LADY BRACKNELL: A country house! . . . You have a town house, I hope? A girl with a simple, unspoilt nature, like Gwendolen, could hardly be expected to reside in the country.

Nonetheless, the image of a happy rural past lingered in town-dwellers' minds: regardless of class, whenever they could, they lived in a house with a garden, and perhaps rented an allotment: they recreated the country in the town while ignoring the reality of its sufferings. Architecture and town-planning increasingly reflected nostalgia for the village, culminating in the Bournville experiment of Cadbury's, the Quaker employers, and in the 'Garden City' movement at the end of the century.

Chapter 13

The Masses and the Classes: The Urban Worker

The urbanization of the mass of the population and the decline of rural areas not surprisingly had profound social consequences for all classes of the population. The greatest fear of the propertied classes in the first half of the century had been of a revolutionary working class or classes: that no such class emerged is perhaps the most striking feature of the second half of the century. Most industrial labourers left no memorial save the products of their labours: the details of their lives, their aspirations, hopes, beliefs, likes, dislikes, habits, and enthusiasms are largely lost. In the empire, detailed reports on all such things were drawn up with all the efficiency of the trained civil servant fascinated by an alien race, but at home it was only at the end of the century that systematic observation of the living customs of the British urban poor began. Mayhew's impressionistic *London Labour and the London Poor: A Cyclopaedia of the Condition and Earnings of Those that Will Work, Those that Cannot Work, and Those that Will not Work* (1861–2) made a start, but an unsystematic one, and one which was only episodically followed up. What we do know suggests highly complex and varied patterns of life, with regionalism and religion often playing an important part.

Rising Wages, Falling Birth-Rate

The standard of living of some members of the labouring population began to increase quite fast. Between 1860 and 1914 real wages doubled. The years of particularly rapid growth were the boom years of 1868–74, and the period 1880–96; during the latter period real wages went up by almost 45 per cent. By the 1880s, for the first time in the century, a significant number began to enjoy leisure time. Some money (though not much) was coming to be available for more than the essentials of food, housing, and clothing.

Strikingly, this surplus coincided not with a rise but with a fall in the birth-rate, which affected the propertied classes from the 1870s, the working classes mirroring their social superiors a little later. The extra cash was thus not absorbed by extra children. This was a startling and unprecedented development which falsified the predictions of the classical political economists from Thomas Malthus to Marx, that the labouring classes were condemned to subsistence levels of living through the 'iron law of wages' because any surplus wealth would be absorbed by extra children. Control of family size opened the way to the relative prosperity of the British working class since the 1880s. How and why this happened is hardly known. Men and women married later; they may have made some use of the rather unreliable birth-control devices popularized from the 1870s; women may have used abortion as a regular means of birth-prevention.

The term 'working classes' (the Victorians almost always used the plural) of course covered a wide spectrum. Charles Booth's survey of *Life and Labour of the People in London*, begun in the late 1880s, found six main categories: 'high-paid labour', 'regular standard earnings', 'small regular earnings', 'intermittent earnings', 'casual earnings', and what Booth called the 'lowest class'. 'Regular standard earners' made up the largest group – as much as the total of the other five categories put together – and it was this group of men and women which particularly reduced the size of their families, saw their real incomes rise, and began to be aware of their potential power within the economy.

Trade Unions

The growing prosperity of the 'regular standard earners' led them to join trade unions as a means of safeguarding their gains and of negotiating for better wages and conditions of work. The unions of the mid-century were for the most part rather narrowly based 'new model' craft unions, made up of men who jealously guarded the privileged and hard-won ascendancy among their fellow employees given them by their qualifications through apprenticeship or their responsibility for skilled machine-working. The steady demand for skilled labour reinforced the influence and status of the craft unions, and some technical developments, for example in the building of iron ships, expanded rather than diminished their importance. In the 1870s and especially in the 1880s these began to be supplemented to include many more of the workmen in regular employment. Rising living standards made this possible, for trade union membership was quite expensive.

The unions existed not only, or even chiefly, for purposes of wage negotiation, but also for a wide variety of 'self-help' benefits and were closely linked to, and sometimes synonymous with, the Friendly Societies. The first of these benefits for any self-respecting workman was the burial benefit – the avoidance of a funeral paid for by the workhouse – but many unions also had sickness and unemployment benefits, for the State as yet offered no help for victims of temporary calamity. Still less did it assist those more permanently disadvantaged, save for the ultimate safety net of the workhouse.

Trade union activity grew in a context which seems most curious to the post-1945 observer. The 20 years after 1874 were characterized by a sharp and substantial deflation – that is, prices (and, to a lesser extent, wages) fell. On the other hand, real wages, for those in regular exployment, rose. But this was hard for trade unionists to come to terms with: a man will hardly believe that an employer who reduces his wages may still be leaving him better off. The 'new unionism' of the 1880s was thus concerned to defend working-class wages: it was a reaction, as much as a positive force. It had little ideology except for the concept of solidarity.

Some socialists played a part in the most publicized strikes of the period – the strike at Bryant and May's match factory in 1888, and the London Dock Strike for the 'dockers' tanner' in 1889, both of which attracted much middle-class interest, probably because they both occurred in London under the noses of the radicals. But these were not typical strikes (indeed the London Dock Strike was not conducted by a union: the union was formed *after* the strike finished); nor should the role of the 'socialists' who led them, such as John Burns, be over-stressed. Most of the trade union leadership remained staunchly Gladstonian: Karl Marx and his works were virtually unknown, outside a small circle, in the country where he had spent almost all his working life; the writings of the socialist groups which sprang up in the 1880s reached only a tiny audience. Indeed, the resistance of the working classes to socialist ideas made them the despair of middle-class intellectuals.

Football and Cricket

If the trade union was the institutional expression of a growing working-class self-awareness, shared leisure activities, especially for the male wage-earner, further encouraged this sense of solidarity. Watching Association Football – a game founded by public schools and university amateur clubs, but essentially professional by the mid-1880s – became the regular relaxation of males (and almost without exception only males) in industrial towns from Portsmouth to Aberdeen. In the last quarter of the nineteenth century a football club was established in every self-respecting industrial town. Some of these teams reflected the religious schisms of the cities (Catholic Celtic and Protestant Rangers in Glasgow, Catholic Everton and Protestant Liverpool on Merseyside). All of them encouraged a local patriotism, enthusiasm, and self-identification on the part of the followers, which was the envy of many a political organizer. Football was the product of a highly organized urban society: the regularity and complexity of the Cup (from 1871) and League (from 1888) competitions, the need for sustained as well as immediate interest, the budgeting for the weekly entrance fee and, perhaps, train fare to the away match, the large, self-regulating crowds, all reflected a disciplined and ordered work-force, content to pay for its leisure watching *others* play for a club organized usually by local businessmen. Sustaining attention on football (or, in the Borders, South Wales, and north England, on rugby) over the 'season' gave the working man something of the wider perspective of time familiar to his agricultural counterpart from the climatic seasons.

The growing popularity of the much lengthier, more idiosyncratic and socially integrative game of cricket, organized through the County Championship from 1873, defies any such simple explanation; it was, perhaps, a testimony to the survival of individuality despite industrialization and the division of labour. W. G. Grace, the Gloucestershire physician whose autocratic command of the pitches and players of the day allowed him to set many batting, bowling, and fielding records still hardly surpassed, became almost as much of a national hero as Fred Archer, the champion jockey in 1874–86. Grace's great and much-caricatured beard caused him to be confused in the popular mind with Lord Salisbury – a confusion probably of some advantage to the latter.

Travel and Betting

Travel for the working class had hitherto taken place in the context of a desperate search for new employment or accommodation. By the 1880s it was starting to be recreational: the trip to the seaside organized individually or by the firm on one of the new Bank Holidays became for many an annual excursion. Resorts – Blackpool, Morecambe,

Scarborough, Southend, Eastbourne, Portobello – rose to meet the demand and to stimulate it further. For the holidays of the working classes were almost always spent in towns: 'the beach' meant the pier, sideshows, and bathing cabins, backed by hotels, boarding houses, and shops. Radicals and socialists in the 1890s attempted to broaden this tradition through rambling and cycling clubs which made trips into the countryside, but the appeal of these was more to the lower middle class than to the working class.

The development of a popular press and the rapid nationwide communication made possible by the electric telegraph encouraged the other great working-class recreation: betting, especially on horses, and, through the nascent pools industry, on football. Betting offered the pot of gold at the end of the rainbow: leisure could be fun, but it might also be profitable – though, of course, it rarely was.

Rising Standards of Living

The more prosperous sections of the working classes thus began to share a little the prosperity and expectations which the industrial revolution had brought the propertied classes half a century earlier. Diets improved a little, with meat, milk, and vegetables in addition to bread, potatoes, and beer. The quality of housing was a little better; houses and people were cleaner as soap became cheaper and generally available. Books, photographs, and the odd item of decorative furniture began to adorn the regularly employed workman's home.
Respectability, in the sense of having the use of money to demonstrate some degree of control of living style, some sense of settled existence, some raising of the horizon beyond the weekly wage packet, became a goal, encouraged by the spread of hire-purchase companies, which managed much of the spending of the working classes' surplus.

The rise in the standard of living of the wage-earning population was important, but it must be kept in perspective. The second half of the nineteenth century was punctuated by short-term dislocations of the economy in each decade. Many contemporaries believed that the years from the mid-1870s to the mid-1890s constituted a 'great depression', when profits fell. As we have seen, this phrase is certainly true with respect to agriculture. With respect to industry as a whole, it was a period of readjustment rather than depression, but for the working person 'readjustment' usually meant misery. It was during the 1880s that the word 'unemployment' was given its modern meaning.

Religion

Religion, in the sense of church-going, played little direct part in the life of most of the urban English. 'It is not that the Church of God has lost the great towns; it has never had them,' wrote A. F. Winnington-Ingram (an Anglican clergyman) in 1896. Protestant Churches both Anglican and nonconformist were unsuccessful in persuading rural labourers to continue as church-goers when they entered the towns, and the Churches failed to reach the majority of those born in towns, despite the indirect allurements of charitable hand-outs and the provision of education in Sunday Schools, and the direct approach of missions, revival crusades, and the Salvation and Church Armies. In London in 1902–3 only about 19 per cent of the population regularly went to church, and those that did came largely from the socially superior areas. The figures would probably be a little better in provincial cities and considerably better in small towns. Only the Roman Catholics attracted significant working-class attendance: their organization was geared to this, and they skilfully appealed through church social organizations and clubs to the Irishness as much as to the Catholicism of their congregations.

The Scots and Welsh continued pious, and the English working classes were not wholly ignorant of religion. 'Rites of passage' (especially weddings and funerals) remained popular even when secular alternatives became available. Nor do non-church-goers appear to have been actively hostile to religion except when it took on a Romish or ritualistic form and became linked with the abrasive relations between Irish immigrants and the host community. Rather, especially in the case of Anglicanism, they resented a religion so obviously linked to the status and power of the propertied classes. Not going to church, in a society whose articulate members so strongly advocated the practice, was a protest as well as a sign of indifference.

Chapter 14
Clerks and Commerce: The Lower Middle Class

For the middle classes, the decades after 1850 offered a golden age of expansion. In 1851 the middle class was a fairly small and reasonably easily identified group: the professions, business men, bankers, large shopkeepers, and the like. The gulf between this group and the working classes was deep. By the end of the century, a far more complex pattern had emerged. A large, intermediate group, which may be called the lower middle class, was called into being by economic change. The service sector of the economy had become much greater and more complex. As the British economy became gradually as much commercial as industrial, it created a vast army of white-collar workers to manage and serve in the retailing, banking, accounting, advertising, and trading sectors.

A New Class

The direction of industrial enterprises started to pass from a paternal family tradition to a new class of professional managers, and the bureaucracies of manufacturing industry grew swiftly. The civil service, both local and central, began to expand rapidly as government spent more on new responsibilities, especially on the education system created by the Act of 1870. Shops, offices, and telephone exchanges offered new opportunities for the employment of women.

London was particularly affected by the changes, which created a vast army of City workers, trained at the new polytechnics, commuting by train or by the new underground railways from the suburbs being built on what was then the edge of the city, or from towns such as Croydon which developed rapidly from the 1870s as dormitories for City clerks. Suburbanization was the characteristic innovation of city life in the second half of the century: rows of neat houses, terraced or semi-detached, with small gardens, often at both front and rear of the house, testified to the successful propertied aspirations of this new society.

Values

These were families which had done well out of the Liberal age: Liberalism called for individual achievement, and this class had responded. It valued merit, competition, respectability, efficiency, and a sense of purpose. It respected achievement, money, and success. Uncertain of its own position in the social order, it responded to those confident of their own right to command: it respected hierarchy. In this, it differed considerably from the sturdy individualism of Liberals in the 1850s, sustained by the pre-industrial ethos of 'the good old cause' and the rallying cries of the seventeenth century; its search for a secure place in the social order made it the vehicle by which the Conservatives became a party with a stake in the cities. In some places, particularly in small towns with a nonconformist tradition such as the market towns of Wales and Scotland, it ran the town, and the self-confidence this gave it, together with its nonconformity, helped to keep it Liberal. In large towns, it tended to act as a collaborating class, offering the aristocracy and the upper middle class the means of power in exchange for recognition and status.

The *Daily Mail*, founded by the Harmsworth brothers in 1896, with its highly efficient national distribution, soon had the provincial press on the run, and was the archetypal reading matter for the lower middle class. Initially liberal-imperialist in tone, it crossed over to the Unionists during the Boer War. 'By office boys for office boys', Lord Salisbury contemptuously remarked of it and its clientele.

Chapter 15
The Propertied Classes

The upper middle classes divided into two. Those working in the professions – doctors, lawyers, the clergy of the established Church, civil servants of the administrative grade – shared a common background of education at university and, increasingly, at one of the public schools. In many towns, they lived more exclusively than in the first half of the century, moving out of the town centre to imposing villas in the suburbs. The habit of sending children away to boarding school increased the national outlook of this class and weakened the roots of its individual members in the localities. The spirit of Arnold of Rugby, as interpreted and modified by his successors, pervaded the outlook of the professions. Educated through a syllabus dominated by Greek, Latin, and ancient history, moralized at by Broad Church Anglicanism, 'fitted for life' by incessant games (rugby football in the winter, cricket and athletics in the summer) designed to occupy every idle moment, the ethos of the professional classes was worthy but sterile. Increasingly designed to provide men to run an empire, it neglected the needs of an industrial state.

The manufacturing middle class was to some extent affected by this. Instead of sending their children early into the family firm, manufacturers increasingly sent them into the educational process designed for the professional classes. Sons of the owners of cotton mills and shipyards learnt Greek and rugby football, and not, as their German counterparts were doing, science and accounting. Sons educated in this way often showed little interest in returning to manufacturing life, and the preservation of the entrepreneurial and manufacturing ethos which had been one of the chief motors of industrial progress in the first half of the century became increasingly difficult. Such men found commerce more congenial than industry, and went into the expanding banking sector where the sweat and gore of the factory floor and labour relations were sterilized into columns of figures.

Financial Services

The British economy came to rely more and more on the competence of such men. A huge balance of payments deficit on imports and exports of commodities began to open (£27 million in 1851, £134 million by 1911). This was turned into an overall surplus by 'invisible earnings' – the profits of banking, insurance, and shipping, and the income from British capital invested abroad. Income from services (£24 million in 1851, £152 million in 1911) and from overseas dividends (£12 million in 1851, £188 million in 1911) seemed to become the vital elements in British prosperity, and with them came a middle class whose chief expertise was in handling money, not men or products.

This important development in British social and economic life was as unplanned as the earlier phase of manufacturing industrialization. It was the product of that industrialization in two ways. As the 'workshop of the world' sold its products abroad, it stimulated other economics which cried out for capital they could not themselves supply. Competition with such economics, and depression in some sectors of manufacturing in the 1880s, lowered the rate of profit on British manufacturing, and the 'invisible hand' thus pointed the way to the expansion of the service industries.

The Absorption of 'Trade'

Again, this tendency must not be exaggerated, nor its novelty over-stressed. The easy fusion of land, industry, and commerce was a well-established English tradition. It had prevented the aristocracy becoming a caste in the Continental style, and it had offered the reward of status to the manufacturer. Some took this reward; others, especially nonconformists, did not seek it. Manufacturing and manufacturers remained a powerful force in England. But the primacy of manufacturers, 'the monarchy of the middle classes', so much expected and feared in the first half of the century, did not occur. In part this must be explained by the extent to which the aristocracy neutralized the political and social effects of 'trade' by absorbing it.

The middle classes were Protestant, and actively so. They were increasingly important within the hierarchy of the Anglican Church and the universities: the latter now catered largely for them, as the passing of professional and civil-service examinations became required through the series of reforms consequent upon the Northcote–Trevelyan Report of 1854. Respectability, the need to maintain the house, and to pay the servants and school and university fees, encouraged restriction in the size of middle-class families from the 1870s; that is, rather earlier than the same phenomenon among the working classes.

Women

Smaller families were also sought by middle-class women, who were beginning to expect more from life than the privilege of breeding children and running the household. Women, thus partially liberated, played an important role in charities, churches, local politics, and the arts, especially music. With great difficulty, some forced themselves upon the universities (they were allowed to attend lectures and take examinations, but not degrees), and from the late 1870s women's colleges were founded at Oxford, Cambridge, and London. The

11. 'The angel in the house'. This rather contrived photograph (1865) reflects a striving for gentility, but also captures something of the loneliness of many middle-class women

professions remained barred to women, but a few succeeded in practising as doctors. The upper levels of nursing and running hotels seemed, however, the nearest most women could get to a professional career.

Chapter 16
Pomp and Circumstance

The aristocracy (and gentry) was only partly affected by these changes. Of the three great classes in British social life, it probably changed the least in Victoria's reign. The aristocracy was, as the socialist writer Beatrice Webb observed, 'a curiously tough substance'. It continued to wield considerable political power, supplying much of the membership of both political parties at Westminster, occupying almost all the upper posts in the empire, running local government in the counties, and officering the army – the navy was less socially exclusive. The aristocracy and gentry gained from prosperous farming in the 1850s–1870s, and lost by the agricultural depression; but it recovered some of its losses by skilful investment in urban land, and by the windfall of urban expansion, when what had been agricultural lands of declining value made their owners wealthy as suburbs were built upon them.

The British aristocracy had always been involved in industrialization, especially in the development of mining, canals, and railways. It now shrewdly associated itself with the new wave of commercial expansion: most banks and insurance companies had a lord to add tone to the managerial board. It also shored up its fortunes by astute marriages, notably with the new aristocracy of wealth in the United States: the best-known example was the marriage of the ninth duke of Marlborough to Consuelo Vanderbilt. By these means, many of the great aristocratic estates were preserved despite agricultural decline.

But they were playthings as much as engines of wealth, and came to be treated as such. The aristocracy came to be known to the urban population chiefly through their representation in the popular press and magazines as men and women of leisure: racing, hunting, shooting, and fishing in the country, gambling and attending the season in London. In a population for which leisure was becoming increasingly important, this did not make the aristocracy unpopular.

The Court

The court led the way. The gravity which Albert applied to court life in the south was applied with equal pertinacity to the serious business of recreation in the north. Victoria and Albert's development of Balmoral on Deeside in the 1850s, their obvious and highly publicized enjoyment of peasant life and lore, and their patronage of Sir Edwin Landseer, the hugely popular artist of rural slaughter, made Scotland respectable, and likewise similar moors and mountains in the north and west of England and in Wales. The court linked itself to the Romantic movement, now in its declining and consequently most popular phase, and by doing so re-established its popularity and represented the control of nature by an urban civilization. *The Monarch of the Glen*, Landseer's portrait of a stag, one of the most reproduced of all Victorian paintings, is not monarch of all he surveys, but a stag at bay, within the gun sights of the stalker: no glen was safe, nature was tamed.

Victoria and Albert's life at Balmoral was enjoyable but high-minded: duty to the peasantry was consistently emphasized. The Prince of Wales, Victoria's son Edward who succeeded her in 1901, was merely hedonistic. A series of scandals alarmed his mother but gratified the press by the copy they yielded. The prince with his coterie of rich friends such as Sir Thomas Lipton, who made a fortune from the new retail trade in groceries, epitomized the 'plutocracy'. The evangelicalism and tractarianism which made such a mark on the aristocracy in post-Regency days, and which made Palmerston's dandyism in the 1850s and

1860s seem conspicuously out of place, appeared to give way to ostentatious consumption and a general moral laxity. Some aristocrats, such as Lord Salisbury, the Tory prime minister, continued the old fashion of simple living despite magnificent surroundings, with a household noted for its religious tone. But Salisbury, the last prime minister to wear a beard, was becoming an anachronism by his last decade, the 1890s. Arthur Balfour, his nephew and successor as prime minister, was seen as a free-thinker. Balfour and Edward VII characterized the new fashion – the one apparently sceptical, the other openly sybaritic.

Despite the marked difference in style between Victoria and her son, the monarchy – the apex of the court and of polite society generally – flourished under both. Victoria in her long reign (1837–1901) jealously guarded its prerogatives, which increasingly she saw as best safeguarded by a Conservative government. Her long disappearances from public life after Albert's death in 1861 were unpopular, and made possible quite a serious republican movement stimulated by the Paris Commune, which was headed off with some skill by the Liberal Party leadership in the early 1870s. It was the absence and idleness of the monarch that caused widespread adverse comment, not her presence. In a rapidly changing society with important elements strongly receptive to the appeal of hierarchy, the monarchy, carefully presented by the growing mass-communications industry, seemed something of a fixed point, with its emphasis on family, continuity, and religion. Walter Bagehot in his classic study, *The English Constitution* (1867), pointed out that the English 'defer to what we may call the *theatrical show* of society . . . the climax of the play is the Queen'. The monarchy helped to legitimize power: it is 'commonly hidden like a mystery, and sometimes paraded like a pageant', as it was with great success at the jubilees in 1887 and 1897. The obvious ordinariness of Victoria herself, her well-publicized sufferings ('the widow of Windsor', bravely performing her duties), and the fact that she was a woman, old and often ill, pointed up the contrast between human frailty and the majesty of institutions, much increasing respect for the latter.

The monarchy represented the timeless quality of what was taken to be a pre-industrial order. In an increasingly urbanized society, it balanced the industrial revolution: the more urban Britain became, the more stylized, ritualized, and popular became its monarchy, for the values which it claimed to personify stood outside the competitive egalitarianism of capitalist society.

Chapter 17
'A Great Change in Manners'

Britain (with the exception of Ireland) between the 1850s and the 1890s was a society of remarkable order and balance, given its extraordinary underlying tensions of industrial and social change. Though political rioting did not altogether disappear, it became infrequent enough to encourage widespread comment. Crime on the mainland, in the form of both theft and acts of violence, declined absolutely as well as relatively – an extraordinary development in a rapidly expanding population, firmly contradicting the adage that industrialization and urbanization necessarily lead to higher rates of criminality. The Criminal Registrar noted in 1901 that, since the 1840s, 'we have witnessed a great change in manners: the substitution of words without blows for blows with or without words; an approximation in the manners of different classes; a decline in the spirit of lawlessness'. This largely self-regulating society relied on voluntary organizations – the Churches, the Friendly Societies, a vast network of charitable organizations – to cater for spiritual and physical deprivation. In one important area – education – it was already admitted by the 1860s that voluntary effort by the Churches could not supply an elementary education system adequate to the needs of an industrial state, and in 1870 the Liberal government passed an act to set up School Boards, with a duty to build board schools where there were no Church schools (though children were not *required* to attend them until 1880, and had to pay to do so until 1891).

Local initiative, especially in London and some of the northern manufacturing towns, grafted on to the elementary schools a quite effective and wide-ranging system of technical education for teenagers and even adults, but because it depended on the imagination of each school board, this system was patchy and in no way matched its German equivalent. Manufacturing towns, notably Manchester and Birmingham, set up civic universities much less oriented towards a classical education than Oxford and Cambridge for those entering the traditional professions. Government responsibility for education was seen by contemporaries as one of Mill's exceptions to the rule, not as the start of a wider acceptance of responsibility for social organization.

Chapter 18
'Villa Tories': The Conservative Resurgence

By increasing the electorate from 20 per cent to 60 per cent of adult men in the towns, and to 70 per cent in the counties, the Reform Acts of 1867 and 1884 posed problems for politicians. Household suffrage presented them with a much larger, though by no means universal, body of voters (far short of a universal suffrage, even for men) and elections were by secret ballot after 1872, whereas previously each individual's vote had been published.

For the Liberal coalition, accustomed never to losing general elections, the question was, could their amorphous system of informal alliances continue to be successful? It was a question posed the more starkly when Gladstone's first government disintegrated in the traditional Liberal style in 1873–4, and then, untraditionally, lost the election, thus yielding power to the Tories for the first time since 1846.

The Liberals' Response

The Liberals' response was twofold. In certain urban areas, and especially in Birmingham, where Joseph Chamberlain was the dominant political figure, a tight 'caucus' system of party organization was introduced. The 'caucus' was a group of self-appointed local notables, often nonconformist business men, and usually strongly critical of the Liberal Party leadership as being too cautious and too aristocratic. The

National Liberal Federation, formed in 1877, attempted to give a degree of bureaucratic unity to the sundry local caucuses. On the other hand, the Liberal leadership, still predominantly aristocratic, reacted with alarm.

Spanning the two groups was the commanding figure of Gladstone, son of a Liverpool (originally Scottish) corn merchant, but educated at Eton and Christ Church, Oxford; himself strongly Anglican but in the later phases of his career sympathetic to nonconformist aspirations, he was thus able to appeal to a wide spectrum of Victorian society. Gladstone had no 'caucus' to back him up: he aspired to a national rather than a local basis of power. He appealed over the heads of the local organizations to the body of Liberal opinion at large, and his means was the political speech and pamphlet.

The new and vast network of national and provincial newspapers, linked by the telegraph, allowed for the first time an instant national debate: a politician's speech could be on the breakfast table of every middle-class household in the land the morning after it was given. Thus in the general election campaign of 1868, in his campaign against the Disraeli government's supine reaction to massacres of Christians by Turks in Bulgaria in 1876, and in his campaign against the moral and financial delinquency of the imperialistic exploits of the Conservatives in 1879–80 (the 'Midlothian Campaign'), Gladstone blazed a new trail in an attempt to create a great popular front of moral outrage. 'The Platform' became the characteristic form of late Victorian politics: Gladstone invented a new forum of political debate, and his contemporaries, both Liberal and Tory, were obliged to join in.

Tory Revival

The 1867 Reform Act brought the Tories new opportunities. Accustomed, almost habituated, to losing, they began to win. In 1867 the National Union of Conservative and Constitutional Associations was founded, and in 1870 a Central Office began to improve the co-ordination of electoral strategy. The target for the Tories was the boroughs: to obtain political power they had to enlarge their base from the counties to the expanding towns and suburbs. This they did with very considerable success in the 1870s and 1880s. Under the leadership of Disraeli they won the general election of 1874 convincingly; under the leadership of Salisbury after Disraeli's death in 1881 they became the predominant party.

They achieved this by linking an essentially hierarchic, aristocratic, and Anglican party with the aspirations of the expanding middle and lower middle classes in the great cities: the Tories became the party of property and patriotism. Disraeli saw that political success was becoming as much a question of presentation as of policy. In famous speeches in Lancashire and at the Crystal Palace in 1872, he portrayed the Liberals as unpatriotic, a danger to property, a threat to the institutions of the nation, betrayers of Britain's world and imperial interests. In a more positive vein, he advocated a policy of social reform, supposedly of particular appeal to such members of the working classes as had recently become voters. The themes of these speeches – especially the patriotic ones – were quickly taken up by other Conservatives. They were the prototype for most Tory election addresses for the next century.

Social Reforms

The early years of the Conservative government of 1874–80 were marked by a burst of social reforms mostly promoted by R. A. Cross, the home secretary: artisans' dwellings, public health, Friendly Societies, river pollution, the sale of food and drugs, merchant shipping, trade unions, factories, drink licensing, and education were all the subject of legislation. Many of these reforms were 'in the pipeline' and owed a strong debt to the Peelite–Liberal traditions which had also motivated the previous Gladstone government. They affected middle-class perhaps more than working-class interests, and because the social measures were permissive rather than compulsory their effect was more limited than might have been expected (for example, by 1880, only 10 of 87 Welsh and English towns had decided to implement the Artisans' Dwellings Act). Nonetheless, these reforms were important in Conservative mythology. They showed that the Tories could be a party which dealt effectively with urban questions, and they offered the basis for the claim that 'Tory democracy' was a reality. Contrasted with German conservative answers to the problems of urban life, they appeared integrative, conciliatory, and constructive.

But the real interest of Conservatism was the consolidation of an urban middle-class base: working-class support was a bonus. The bogy of Liberal lack of patriotism was only partially successful, for the Tories' claim to be the party of competent imperialism was severely dented by their mishandling of events in South Africa and Afghanistan in the late 1870s, and by the high costs of their military exploits. It was hard simultaneously to be imperialists and to appeal to the middle-class virtue of financial retrenchment: a self-contradiction which Gladstone's Midlothian speeches skilfully exposed.

The Nadir of Liberalism

The Tories lost the 1880 general election, borne down partly by Gladstone's oratory, partly by the trade recession of that year. The succeeding Gladstone government of 1880–5 was the nadir of Liberalism, the party restless, the Cabinet divided. In imperial affairs, Tory claims seemed borne out: hesitation and confusion led to a series of disasters, culminating in the death of Charles Gordon at Khartoum in 1885. Too habituated to the way the 'official mind' of the colonial office thought to decline to extend imperial responsibilities, the Liberals occupied territory while declaring their regrets: electorally, they lost both ways, alienating anti-imperialists by doing too much, and imperialists by seeming reluctant.

12. Gladstone on the stump, addressing a crowd in Warrington, Lancashire, from his election train in 1885

In domestic affairs, Gladstone's determination to control and reduce expenditure made positive reform difficult. In marked contrast to 1868–74, the government was noted for only one great reform, the county franchise reform of 1884. The enfranchisement of agricultural labourers was expected to deliver the county seats into the Liberals' hands, and Salisbury used the blocking power of the House of Lords to extract a great prize as a 'tit-for-tat': a redistribution bill allowed the boundaries of borough seats to be drawn much more favourably to the Tories. Thus the Tories were able to use a Liberal reform to create a political structure of single-member, middle-class urban and suburban constituencies, on which the basis of their subsequent political success rested for over a century.

The effect of this was to make the Liberals increasingly dependent on the 'Celtic fringe', the Irish, Scottish, and Welsh MPs. The concerns and priorities of these three countries thus moved on to the centre of the British imperial stage.

Chapter 19
Ireland, Scotland, Wales: Home Rule Frustrated

That there was an 'Irish problem', nobody could deny: what it was, hardly anybody could agree. Disraeli caught the tone of metropolitan bewilderment: 'I want to see a public man come forward and say what the Irish question is. One says it is a physical question; another, a spiritual. Now it is the absence of the aristocracy, then the absence of railroads. It is the Pope one day, potatoes the next.'

Irish Agriculture

Irish agriculture was overwhelmingly the country's largest industry and was overwhelmingly owned by Protestants, who mostly, contrary to popular myth, lived on or near their estates. It flourished in the boom of the 1850s and 1860s and achieved a modest degree of technical improvement, but it remained, compared with England, grossly under-capitalized. Ireland could not produce its own capital, and could not attract much from England. The Irish economy could not sustain its population: unknown numbers moved to the mainland, where no town of any size was without its Irish community. Between 1841 and 1925 gross 'overseas' emigration included 4.75 million to the USA, 70,000 to Canada, and more than 370,000 to Australia.

Fenians and Parnellites

The legacy of the 1798 rebellion, the failure of Daniel O'Connell's attempt in the 1830s and 1840s to repeal the 1800 Act of Union, and the catastrophe of the Famine of 1845–6 and 1848, produced the Fenian Irish independence movement of the 1860s, which attempted risings in the USA, Canada, and Ireland. In 1867 it astonished England by a series of bomb explosions, notably one at Clerkenwell Prison in London, in which over 100 innocent persons were killed. The Fenian movement in no sense represented Irish opinion generally, but the danger that it might come to do so encouraged Liberal politicians, especially Gladstone, to concessionary action. Disestablishment of the Anglican Church in Ireland in 1869, the Land Act of 1870, and an abortive university reform in 1873 (rejected by the Irish members themselves) were intended to show that Westminster could give the mass of the Irish what they wanted. But these reforms were not enough. Isaac Butt's Home Government Association flourished, and the Liberal Party, hitherto the dominant party in Irish politics, was on the run. The agricultural depression from the early 1870s to the mid-1890s greatly worsened the situation.

Charles Stewart Parnell (like Butt, a Protestant) became leader of the Home Rule Party in 1877, a position he held until his ruin in a divorce scandal in 1890. Parnell was prepared to exploit every political situation without reluctance or embarrassment – but even this tougher line was to some extent outflanked by the Land League, which sought personal ownership of the land for the peasantry. Parnell, somewhat ambivalently, became its president in 1879. The Land League – a potent blend of 'physical-force' Fenians and 'moral-force' Parnellites fused into a popular front of nationalistic Catholicism – fought a sustained campaign against evictions in the 'Land War' of 1879–82 at the height of the depression, meeting them with violence and their perpetrators with 'boycotting' (named after Captain Charles Boycott, whose nerve cracked when faced with social and economic ostracism). Violence in the Irish countryside, and the murder in 1882 of the Irish secretary, Lord Frederick Cavendish, Gladstone's nephew by marriage, astonished and appalled the propertied classes in England, which, as we have seen, had become accustomed to a very low level of violent crime.

Home Rule

The Gladstone government of 1880 met this crisis on the one hand with coercion and on the other with concession, in the form of the 1881 Land Act, which gave much to the peasants, but did not give them ownership. The Home Rule Party increased its hold on Ireland (helped by the county franchise reform of 1884) and at the election of December 1885 won 86 seats, thus holding the balance of power between the Liberals and Tories at Westminster.

Gladstone cut the Gordian knot by coming out for Home Rule; a private appeal to Salisbury to treat the question on a bipartisan basis was rejected. Gladstone's decision was quite consistent with the main thrust of Liberal thinking, but its timing recognized political necessity: only once subsequently, in 1906, were the Liberals to gain power without the need for the support of Home Rule MPs in the lobbies. Most Liberals championed devolution and the rights of nations 'struggling rightly to be free', as Gladstone put it; it was hard to deny in 1886 that Ireland had proved itself to be such a nation. The question was, was its nationality to be recognized or crushed? Moreover, the moderate Home Rule Bill produced by Gladstone in 1886 did not grant independence, though it was the argument of its opponents, first, that despite Parnell's assurances it would in the long run lead to Irish independence, and, second, that it gave no safeguard against 'Rome Rule' to the Protestant population, mostly concentrated in Belfast, the industrial capital of the province of Ulster.

This complex series of events led to a major crisis in British politics. The Liberal Party, faced with Gladstone's Home Rule Bill in the summer of

1886, split: 93 MPs, most of them Whigs under Lord Hartington but with some radicals under Joseph Chamberlain, voted with the Tories against the bill, thus bringing down the Liberal government and introducing 20 years of Conservative (or Unionist, as the anti-Home Rule Coalition was called) hegemony. With the Liberal-Unionists (the defectors from Liberalism) went a significant proportion of the Liberal press and almost all those landed aristocrats who traditionally paid most of the party's electoral expenses. This loss of influence and money was probably of more importance to the Liberals than the actual numbers of defecting MPs, though in the Lords the Liberals were now a tiny minority.

The split of 1886 weakened the party, but left Gladstone in control of it and of the National Liberation Federation, a hold he consolidated at its Newcastle meeting in 1891 when he accepted its radical programme. Home Rule thus shackled Liberalism to Gladstone. Before 1886, Ireland blocked the way to the passage of second-rank measures, so Home Rule was necessary as well as right. But after 1886, Home Rule was impossible, given the existence of the House of Lords. Home Rule thus both stimulated Liberals to battle for the right, and condemned them to a generation of frustration.

Scotland and Wales

Naturally enough, events in Ireland affected Scotland and Wales. In both, disestablishment of the Church also became a political issue, and both experienced land campaigns. These had little of the violence characteristic of parts of Ireland, though in the Isle of Skye troops were used in 1882 to suppress crofter demonstrations. Certain Liberals in both countries demanded 'Home Rule All Round' and this movement, buoyed up by the cultural renaissance that Wales and Scotland shared with Ireland in the late nineteenth century, achieved considerable influence in the Liberal Party in the late 1880s and 1890s. Unlike Ireland, however, the Liberal Party was able to contain within itself the quasi-nationalistic movements in Scotland and Wales, partly because the dominant industrial sector in Scotland and the growing predominance in Wales of the South Wales coalfield bound those countries far more intimately than Ireland to the imperial economy; in southern Scotland and south Wales, Liberal imperialism trumped nationalism.

Tory Consolidation

With the Liberal Party split, and unable to reunite despite various attempts in the late 1880s, the Tories consolidated their hold. They were not active reactionaries. Salisbury made no attempt to reverse the Liberal achievements of the 1850s–1870s, which at the time he had so bitterly opposed. Their position and their alliance with the Liberal-Unionists depended on preventing things being done, not on doing them. Thus though some legislation was passed, particularly the establishment of elected County Councils in 1888, a measure to improve working-class housing in 1890, and, later, the Education Act of 1902, which went some way to establishing a system of secondary education, the Unionist hegemony of 1886–1905 was not a period of legislative significance, nor was it intended to be.

The urban electorate which the Tories essentially relied upon wanted the continuation of the Liberal state of the 1850s and 1860s, without the new accretions to Liberalism such as Home Rule. It rejected Gladstonian Liberalism, not because it had turned its back on the gains of the free-trade years in the mid-century, but because the Gladstonian Liberals seemed to have progressed too far beyond the objectives of that period. The anti-Gladstonian coalition thus relied heavily on Home Rule to keep the coalition together and to keep the Liberals out. It ventured beyond its anti-Home Rule stance at its electoral peril, as it was to find out in the early years of the twentieth century.

The continuing Liberal commitment to Home Rule helped in this. The short Liberal minority government of 1892–5 (Gladstone's last administration, with the Earl of Rosebery as its prime minister after

Gladstone's retirement in 1894) spent much effort upon the second Home Rule Bill, which it succeeded in passing through the Commons only to see it thrown out by the Lords. The Liberals could mount a disparate majority made up of the English counties, Scotland, Wales, and Ireland, but they could not sustain it or repeat it. The Unionists won convincingly in 1895 and confirmed their majority in 1900, taking advantage of temporary successes in the South African war to hold the 'Khaki election'.

Chapter 20
Reluctant Imperialists?

The Unionist case against Home Rule had always had an imperial
dimension: imperial power must not be devolved, the very
circumstances of the passing of the Act of Union in 1800 showing the
strategic importance of Ireland, which Home Rule would again put at
risk. In the last third of the century, imperial issues became much more
of a public preoccupation; we must now look at their effect on Britain's
position in the world.

Trade and the Flag

The British did not as a whole look for increased direct imperial
authority, and pressure groups for its extension were of little popular or
political significance. Indeed, in the old areas of white settlement, they
successfully sought to devolve authority, passing the Dominion of
Canada Act in 1867 and the Commonwealth of Australia Act in 1900. Yet
the last 40 years of the century saw the annexation of vast areas of land
in Africa, the Far East, and the Pacific. In 1851 Britain was the world's
trader, with an overwhelming dominance of world shipping, which
continued even when Britain's dominance in manufactured goods was
declining after 1870. British interests were thus to be found wherever
there was trade, even though British imperial authority might not be
formally present. *Informal* imperialism thus preceded formal annexation:
nothing could be less true than the adage, 'trade follows the flag'. In

almost every case, it was the opposite. As Joseph Conrad's novels illustrate, there was no creek, however distant, without its British representative, organizing the shipping of paraffin oil and local goods.

In East and Central Africa, the first European presence was often religious, as evangelical medical missionaries such as David Livingstone preached the gospel, healed the sick, and exposed the inhumanity of the inland slave trade. H. N. Stanley's 'rescue' of Livingstone in 1871, skilfully self-publicized, became one of the great adventure stories of Victorian times, and greatly increased interest in 'the dark continent'.

In some areas, British attempts to trade were supported by arms – a notable example being the opium monopoly of the Indian government and the general free-trading access which was forced upon the Chinese government by the British in a series of 'opium wars', culminating in the treaty of Tien-tsin (1858), the most disreputable of all Britain's imperialistic exploits, because it was a considered and consistent policy, not the accidental result of a local crisis. Governmental involvement of an oblique sort was sometimes used to develop small beginnings through the device of the Chartered Company – a trading company with governmentally guaranteed rights to trade and administer an area; Nigeria, East Africa, and Rhodesia all came under eventual British rule in this way, for when a Company went bankrupt (or effectively so – Cecil Rhodes's British South Africa Company never paid a dividend before 1920 and was taken over in 1923), the British government had little option but to assume its administrative responsibilities.

India

In addition to this huge and largely informal network of trade was the centre-piece of India, 'the chief jewel in the imperial crown', now no longer so profitable, but the assumed focal point of British thinking about security outside the European context. Following the Indian mutiny of 1857–8, the old East India Company was wound up, and its

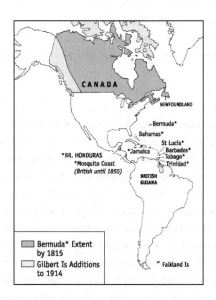

Map 4. The expansion of the British Empire, 1815–1914

territories came under direct British administration. In 1876, at the express wish of the queen, an Act was passed at Westminster which declared her 'empress of India'.

To safeguard India, and the route to that subcontinent, various annexations were made. In the vicinity, Burma and Malaya were annexed, largely at the urging of the government of India in Calcutta, which conducted its own programme of imperialism with the systematic approach characteristic of everything it did, and quite dissimilar to the haphazard methods of London. On the route, Egypt and the Sudan came under British control, and imperial expansion in East and South Africa was at least partly affected by Indian considerations. This simple statement of course disguises an extremely complex narrative with respect to each of these annexations. The most

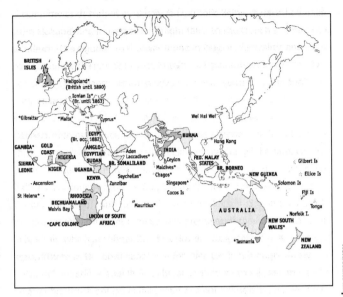

controversial annexations were in Egypt and South Africa, and some
attention should be given to these.

The Crimea

The route to India had made security in the eastern Mediterranean,
especially against Russia, a long-standing British preoccupation.
Between 1854 and 1856 the British and French, with some assistance
from Piedmont–Sardinia, had sent substantial fleets and armies to prop
up Turkey. The Crimean War had a complex series of causes, but the
root one was Russian aggrandizement against the sprawling and feeble
Ottoman Empire. The performance of Britain and France, the two most
'advanced' European nations, against 'backward' Russia was
disappointing and in certain respects inept, although the supply by sea

121

of large armies at a considerable distance created new problems. The newspaper reporting by telegraph of the hardships of the troops starkly illustrated the problems and the paradox of warmaking by a liberal state, and Florence Nightingale made a name for herself as the 'lady with the lamp'. The immobility of the campaign, which consisted largely of a series of sieges, bloodily resolved in the Crimea and in the area of Kars in Asiatic Turkey, looked forward to the 1914–18 war. Turkey was successfully defended, and the British thus shored up the Ottoman Empire, of which Egypt was a part.

Turkey

The hope was that Turkey would reform and behave like a modern, liberal state. This hope was not fulfilled. By the 1870s, Turkey was again disintegrating, and under attack from Russia. The Disraeli government of 1874–80 continued the Crimean policy of defending Turkish integrity. The Liberal opposition under Gladstone argued that this was no longer feasible and supported the division of much of 'Turkey in Europe' into separate, Christian states. The 'Concert of Europe' present at the Congress of Berlin in 1878 reached agreement on this, and Disraeli returned to London bringing 'peace with honour' and the imperial gain of the island of Cyprus, thought to be of strategic importance for the eastern Mediterranean, but in fact useless as a naval base.

Egypt

As Turkey disintegrated, so Egypt became increasingly self-reliant, organizing the building of the Suez Canal, opened in 1869, and of great importance to Britain's links with India. The inflow of capital to build the canal destabilized Egypt, which began to disintegrate socially and politically. In 1875 Disraeli bought the Khedive's large holding in the shares of the company which ran the canal. Thus when Egypt reached the point of bankruptcy, and a military coup was attempted, Britain had not only a general strategic interest in the situation but also a direct financial one. After attempts to find alternatives, Gladstone reluctantly invaded and occupied Egypt on behalf of the canal's creditors in 1882, and the British remained until 1954, though the country was never formally annexed and was thus similar in status to the theoretically independent princely states in India. Formal annexation of the rebellious Sudan naturally followed in a series of campaigns in the 1880s and 1890s, the Mahdi, the slayer of the maverick Gordon in 1885, being finally and ruthlessly crushed by Field Marshal Kitchener at the battle of Omdurman in 1898. Turkish decay thus drew Britain into becoming the major power in the eastern Mediterranean and in north-eastern Africa.

South Africa

Events in South Africa were not dissimilar, but were complicated by the presence of the Boers. The Cape was occupied in 1795 to safeguard the route to India. The security of the hinterland, whither the Boers had trekked in the 1830s, affected the Cape. Various plans for incorporating the Boers in a federation were suggested, and confederation was imposed upon the Boers by the Disraeli government in 1877 at a moment when the Boers were weakened by the Zulus. Incompetent generalship (a feature of British military operations in South Africa) led to the death of 800 British troops at Isandhwana, one of the very few occasions in colonial wars in which spears triumphed over guns. This was, of course, only a temporary set-back, and the Zulus were liquidated at Ulundi (1879). The Boers then wished to regain their independence. After a short war, when the defeat of a small group of British soldiers at Majuba Hill in 1881 gave a propaganda coup to the Boers out of all proportion to its military significance, an ill-defined agreement was reached: the Transvaal and Orange Free State to have independence, but under British suzerainty.

Increasing exploitation of diamonds and the discovery of gold in the Transvaal in 1886 transformed the situation. In financial terms, Southern

Africa became literally Britain's chief imperial jewel. The influx of capital directed by men such as Cecil Rhodes destabilized the rural economy of the Boers, as it had that of Egypt. The Transvaal, like Egypt, went bankrupt, but the Boers, under Paul Kruger, retained strict political control. An attempt by Dr Jameson, a crony of Rhodes, to encourage a rising by the Uitlanders (the British in the Transvaal without political rights) failed in 1896. Alfred Milner, the new high commissioner, asserted British rights over the Boer republics and determined to break Kruger by war. Milner goaded Kruger into attacking Cape Colony in 1899, and what was expected to be a short, limited war began. The Boers, however, were well stocked with German arms; the British, used to fighting colonial wars against undisciplined natives without guns, proceeded ineptly, and a series of disasters followed before weight of armaments captured the main Boer cities in 1900. The war seemed over, and Chamberlain, the colonial secretary, persuaded Salisbury to hold the 'Khaki election', easily won by the Unionists. But the Boers refused to accept defeat, and harassed the British with guerrilla tactics. The British replied by burning Boer farms, clearing the veldt, and systematically herding Boer families into 'concentration camps'. High death-rates in the camps led to radical protests in Britain. 'When is a war not a war?' asked Sir Henry Campbell-Bannerman, Rosebery's successor as Liberal leader, answering himself: 'When it is carried on by methods of barbarism in South Africa.' In 1902, peace was negotiated: Milner had failed in his aim of smashing the social and political structure of Afrikanerdom.

Chapter 21

The *Fin-de-Siècle* Reaction: New Views of the State

The Boer War was immensely expensive, costing far more than all Britain's other imperial exploits in the nineteenth century put together. It failed to smash the Boers, but it did smash the Gladstonian system of finance, raising government expenditure to a new plateau from which it never descended. The war also put into stark and dramatic popular form a number of concerns which were already preoccupying the intelligentsia. The war showed the strength and loyalty of the empire, for the white colonies sent troops to help, but it also showed its weaknesses. The empire seemed over-extended and under-co-ordinated. The British navy was no longer pre-eminent. The French navy was being joined as a threat by the Germans, the Italians, the Americans, and the Japanese. The policy of 'splendid isolation' began to look dangerous.

Imperial rivalry had meant that in the 1870s–1890s France had usually seemed Britain's most likely enemy and Germany the most likely friend. Germany's navy plan of 1898, and its bid for 'a place in the sun', which coincided with its encouragement to Kruger during the Boer War, now made Germany seem a potent threat, the contemporary feeling about which is well captured in Erskine Childers's classic spy story *The Riddle of the Sands* (1903). Naval security in the Indian Ocean and the Pacific was gained by the Anglo-Japanese alliance of 1902. This attempt to limit imperial responsibility was followed up by agreements (*ententes*) resolving imperial differences with France in 1904 over North Africa and with Russia in 1907 over Persia. The Boer War thus led to a 'new course' in British foreign policy. For while these *ententes* were formally about extra-European areas, their real importance came to lie within Europe; although they were not alliances, they committed Britain, to some extent, to the side of the Franco-Russian alliance against Germany and Austria in the rising tension in Europe. What that extent was, it was not yet clear.

The Economy

Anxieties about world security raised by the Boer War also popularized discussion about Britain's relative economic position, for it was upon this that national strength ultimately rested. The overwhelming superiority of the British economy of the 1850s was much diminished. The USA, Germany, France, and Russia were now all substantial industrial powers, with the first two superior to the British in certain sectors of their economies. Britain was now one among several, no longer the unaccompanied trail-blazer. Yet for the most part British society and government behaved as if nothing had changed. The liberal state of the 1850s and 1860s, with its precepts of free trade, minimal government spending, and an economy autonomous and self-regulating, lingered on, almost as carefully guarded under Conservative as under Liberal management. The *per capita* expenditure of central government in 1851 was £2.00; by 1891 it had only increased to £2.50 (by 1913 it was to be £4.00). In the 1880s and 1890s this situation came under increasing criticism, much of which the Boer War seemed to confirm and popularize.

Slow military progress in the Crimean War of the 1850s led to criticism of the competence of the ruling elite; military ineffectiveness and the poor quality of recruits in the South African war led to a public cry among the propertied classes for a reappraisal of the economic, social, and even political arrangements of the nation as a whole.

Social Darwinism

Before considering the various schools of criticism of traditional Liberalism, a general influence should be noted: that of 'social Darwinism'. We saw earlier that positivists were strong supporters of *laissez-faire*. In the 1880s and 1890s the influence of social Darwinism began to take a different form. The struggle for 'the survival of the fittest' began to be seen less in terms of individuals in the market-place and more in terms of competition between nations. This dramatically reduced the number of units under discussion, and raised the question, prompted also by the imperialism which was related to this national competition, of whether individual 'races' were not better subjects for inquiry than a myriad of individuals, and whether 'advanced races' could control their destinies by governmental, social, or perhaps even genetic organization.

This concept – a marrying of the British science of evolution and the German concept of the organic state – powerfully affected contemporary thought: the language of 'race' became the common coin of reformers right across the political spectrum, from Rudyard Kipling, ostensibly the poet of the right, through J. A. Hobson and L. T. Hobhouse, the philosophers of the new liberals, to G. B. Shaw, regarded as the playwright of the left. The popular form of social Darwinism readily became a facile assumption of racial superiority, linked to imperialism, as the popular press reported the successes of the many small-scale colonial military expeditions. Popular reporting of these emphasized the importance of individual daring, character, and initiative, 'deeds that won the empire', rather than the enormous technical disparity between a disciplined European army armed with rifles, and from the 1890s the occasional machine-gun, and local forces relying on massed use of spears or, at best, sporadic musket fire.

'National Efficiency'

Criticism of the liberal state in its classic Victorian form came from three chief political directions: from discontented Conservatives and Unionists who believed their political leadership was excessively hidebound by the canons of Peel–Gladstone fiscal policy, from Liberals who believed Liberalism must move on to meet new challenges, and from socialists who, at least at first glance, challenged the whole order of the state. Elements from each of these came together to demand 'national efficiency', a slogan intended to suggest a willingness to use government power to organize and legislate for an 'Imperial race' fit to meet the challenges of the world.

Critics of the Free-Trade State

The free-trade state had always had its critics. The most influential of these in the second half of the nineteenth century was John Ruskin, art critic and social commentator. Politically impossible to categorize, Ruskin's powerful prose in works such as *Unto this Last* (1862) attacked the aesthetics of industrial society, but he offered no very systematic critique. His aesthetic criticisms were taken up by the Pre-Raphaelite Brotherhood, a group of painters, writers, and craft workers who emphasized, especially through the writings and designs of William Morris, the values of pre-industrial England, a mythical land of craft workers, contented peasants, and romance. From such influences sprang wide-ranging changes in design and architecture, epitomized by the 'English style' of domestic architecture of Norman Shaw and, at the turn of the century, Edwin Lutyens, which characterized the best of the building of the new suburbs. From Morris also sprang a socialist rhetoric of enduring potency: the image of a rural, self-sufficient, egalitarian society of sturdy yeomen. Morris did not confront industrialization, he by-passed it.

The aestheticism of the Pre-Raphaelites, and their general critique of middle-class morality, was given fresh impetus by the aesthetes of the 1880s and 1890s, the most notable of whom was the wit and playwright Oscar Wilde. He was ruined, like his fellow Irishman Parnell, by the public exposure of his sexual habits. Wilde's remarkable essay, 'The Soul of Man under Socialism', exemplified the links between aestheticism and individualist rather than collectivist socialism.

The Left

From 1884 these leanings towards socialism were supplemented by the London-based Fabian Society, whose members included Sidney and Beatrice Webb, Shaw, H. G. Wells, and, later, the young Ramsay MacDonald, all strong social evolutionists. The Fabians' criticism of the Liberal economic order was not so much that it was unjust, as that it was inefficient and wasteful: a centrally planned economy and labour market, administered by an elite of trained professionals, would eliminate inefficiency, the trade cycle, and its by-products such as unemployment and poverty. It would attain this end gradually through legislation and not by revolution (hence the name Fabian, after the Roman general whose tactics the society emulated).

Perhaps the chief contribution of the Fabians was to assist in the development of a fresh concept of 'progress' on the British left, which in the 1880s was becoming limited in its horizons by the persistent wrangles over Home Rule. For the Fabians addressed themselves to the existing intelligentsia: they were not a popular movement. But popular discontent with the limitations of Gladstonian Liberalism was also developing; Keir Hardie, a former coalminer from the Ayrshire coalfield, stood for the view that the increasingly unionized working class must have its own representatives in the House of Commons (where MPs were still not paid). Hardie, elected for West Ham in 1892, had helped form the Scottish Labour Party in 1888 and, in 1893, founded the Independent Labour Party in Bradford. The ILP saw itself as a socialist party, but it had difficulty in establishing a popularly supported organization. It shared with the Liberals an anti-imperialist rhetoric, supported 'Home Rule All Round', but called also for nationalization. H. M. Hyndman's Social Democratic Federation was more vigorous in its quasi-Marxist ideology, but gained very little popular foothold.

Chapter 22
Old Liberalism, New Liberalism, Labourism, and Tariff Reform

All these movements were limited in their impact; the Liberals remained overwhelmingly the dominant party of the 'left' (the use of the word became common in British political discussion for the first time in the 1880s). Nonetheless, the ideas being put forward, and the threat of their organizational success, concentrated Liberal minds.

Land Reform

Liberals made their own contribution to the intellectual debates of the last two decades of the century. Always the party of land reform, their enthusiasm for it was rekindled by works such as the American Henry George's *Progress and Poverty* (1880). Posing the question, 'what *does* produce poverty amid advancing wealth?', George's answer was, crudely stated, the rents of the landed proprietor and the exclusion of workmen from free access to land, both rural and urban. The solution was a thoroughgoing and efficient land tax, known as 'the single tax'. The land campaign was a major theme of radicalism until the First World War, and beyond.

'Why do we sit and quietly behold degradation worse than that from which we have rescued women and children in mines and factories?' asked Arnold Toynbee, the liberal Christian historian and radical and, with T. H. Green, a great radical influence in the Oxford of the 1870s and early 1880s. Toynbee's followers (such as Canon Barnett, founder of Toynbee Hall in East London in 1884) encouraged, first, personal (often religious) commitment on the part of the intelligentsia to on-the-spot observation of working-class problems, and, second and later, an acceptance that voluntary effort would not be sufficient by itself to solve those problems.

New Liberalism

'Advanced radicals' came to anticipate much greater government involvement in the economy, and much more 'positive liberalism' to see that each individual had the means by which he or she could make the most of his or her individual abilities. This was bound to cost money, and Liberals believed this money should be raised by increasing direct taxation, in particular death duties and a graduated income tax, to achieve a measure of redistribution at the same time as raising revenue. An important step in this direction was taken by the 1892–5 minority Liberal government, which paid for increased social reform and naval expenditure by imposing for the first time an effective death duty.

'New Liberalism', as this movement came to be called, was an attempt to justify the free-market system by making it work 'fairly'; it attempted a rationalization of capitalism, not its replacement. The movement, whose most effective author was J. A. Hobson, also a strong critic of 'immoral' imperialism, hoped to convert the Liberal Party to 'New Liberalism' and thus to allow the continuation of the Liberals as a broadly based party, capable of continuing to assimilate and integrate the urban working class. This would avoid the German situation, where the working class had formed its own class-based Marxist party which rejected the legitimacy of the German State. This view was reinforced by political expediency on the Liberals' part. Following a series of adverse legal decisions which questioned their legal right to picket and their freedom from damages culminating in the famous Taff Vale case

(1900–1), some trade unions, now in the late 1890s growing fast, joined with the ILP to form the Labour Representation Committee in 1900. The Liberals, split three ways by the Boer War, were at their weakest, and seemed to be able to offer the trade unionists, hitherto Liberal, little chance of redress. The secretary of the LRC, Ramsay MacDonald, negotiated an electoral agreement with the Liberals in February 1903, by which Liberal and Labour constituency parties would not split the progressive vote to let in a Unionist, but would reach local agreements by which a number of Labour candidates would have a good chance of being elected.

This accommodation between the two parties of the left showed the considerable area of agreement that existed between them: the Labour Party (as the LRC became in 1906) was part of the 'party of progress', at least for the time being, sharing many of its reforming aspirations, and its commitment to free trade.

Tariff Reform

The Unionists (as the coalition of Tories and Liberal-Unionists should be called after 1895, when Joseph Chamberlain and Lord Hartington, the Liberal-Unionist leaders, entered Salisbury's Cabinet) wished to conserve the British constitution as it then stood. But most of them also conserved its fiscal arrangements and remained free traders. Lord Salisbury gave no effective support to protection despite his large majority in both Houses. The imperialist faction within his party, however, increasingly came to see some form of imperial protection as essential.

Their reasons for this were threefold. First, they believed that the growing success of the American and German economies was due to the protection of young industries, and that in the new era of technically sophisticated industry – chemicals, electricals, cars – Britain would lose out unless there was protection, a degree of planning, and

13. Joseph Chamberlain's Tariff Reform Campaign assaulting the free-trade tradition, as caricatured by F. Carruthers Gould in the *Westminster Gazette*, 12 November 1903

much more co-operation between industry and education, all things that only government could supervise. Second, they believed that an Imperial Customs Union (analogous to the German *Zollverein* of the early nineteenth century) could integrate the empire's economy, Britain producing manufactured goods, the colonies raw materials. Third, they saw tariffs, including duties on food, as the only alternative to direct taxation to pay for the social reforms necessary to make the imperial race fit for the increasingly harsh competition between nations which they believed the future would bring.

This programme was embodied in the Tariff Reform campaign launched by Joseph Chamberlain in 1903 while still colonial secretary, much to the embarrassment of the prime minister, Arthur Balfour, who had succeeded his uncle, Lord Salisbury, the previous year. Well financed, sophisticatedly organized and presented, Tariff Reform divided the Unionist Party (though the young Winston Churchill was one of the few

MPs who actually left it). It was renounced by the electorate in a series of by-elections and then in the general election of 1906, when the Liberals together with 29 Labour MPs returned with a huge overall majority. England had turned from Home Rule in the 1880s and 1890s, but not from free trade. The Peel–Gladstone tradition of open markets and cheap food still carried great weight: 'the big loaf and the little loaf' was the Liberals' effective catch-phrase.

The End of Victorianism

But although the 1906 Liberal success was the result mainly of negative factors – hostility to Tariff Reform, the dislike of Balfour's 1902 Education Act by nonconformists (their ranks swollen by a great religious revival), general criticism of the Unionists' handling of imperial affairs – the atmosphere had changed. There was much 'old Liberalism' (and 'old Toryism') still around, but the critiques of the Victorian liberal state made from the left, the right, and by Liberals themselves bit deep.

The opening years of the twentieth century (there was much debate as to whether it began on 1 January 1900 or 1901) brought the widespread use by the better-off of its characteristic appliances, available in the 1890s but slow to find markets because of technical inadequacies – electric light in the houses, telephones, typewriters, gramophones, cars – and, soon, wireless and aeroplanes. The first building in the world specially designed as a cinema was opened in Colne, Lancashire, in 1907. Quite suddenly, the Victorian years and their preoccupations began to seem worlds away. The deaths of the three most notable public figures of those years – Gladstone in 1898, Victoria herself in 1901, Salisbury in 1903 – emphasized the change.

Chapter 23

Edwardian Years: A Crisis of the State Contained

Reappraisals of the nineteenth-century state were reinforced by a series of social inquiries in the 1890s and early 1900s into the working of the labour market and into social conditions – investigations such as Charles Booth's *Life and Labour of the People in London* (which appeared in four series of 33 volumes in all, 1889–1903) and Seebohm Rowntree's *Poverty: A Study of Town Life* (1901). Booth and Rowntree for the first time attempted to define 'poverty' as a social phenomenon (as opposed to the Poor Law's definition of pauperism, which was a legal category). Rowntree found over 27 per cent of the population of York living in what he called 'primary or secondary poverty'. Standards of living might have risen for employed working people since the 1880s, but a significant proportion of the population was shown still to live in 'poverty' (a relative term) and on the brink of economic disaster. This contrasted markedly with the flamboyant 'plutocratic' living, noted earlier, of some members of the court and aristocracy.

Almost 30 per cent living in poverty was shocking, and it shocked contemporaries. But it also meant that 70 per cent were living in relative affluence, a proportion inconceivable in the days of the 'iron law of wages' of the mid-century. In the 1860s, Gladstone as chancellor had admitted that the economy necessarily functioned with an 'enormous mass of paupers', and Victorians had been aware, in an ill-defined and helpless way, of the waste and suffering around them. Matthew

14. The residuum. A mother and child in Glasgow, c.1910, an unusual early flash photograph of one of Rowntree's 10 per cent living in primary poverty

Arnold's *Culture and Anarchy* (1869) described London's East End as containing 'those vast, miserable, unmanageable masses of sunken people'. Victorian reactions to it had been consequently local and personal, in the form of personal, charitable endeavour to alleviate the lot of those actually known to them or of particular categories of the so-called 'deserving poor'; for example, distressed gentlefolk. Now, at the turn of the century, systematic investigation not only raised alarm that an 'imperial race' could be so impoverished, but, by providing figures, suggested manageability and means of redress: until the scale of the problem was known, it could not be tackled. 'While the problem of 1834 was the problem of pauperism, the problem of 1893 is the problem of poverty', remarked Alfred Marshall, the leading free-trade economist; he implied that the problem of poverty had become both definable and solvable.

Poverty and the State

The Liberal governments of 1905–14, especially after Herbert Asquith became prime minister in 1908 on Campbell-Bannerman's death, made a considerable attempt to begin to come to terms with these questions. Free school meals (1907); old age pensions (a scheme drawn up in 1908 by Asquith before becoming prime minister, though seen through the Commons by David Lloyd George, his successor as chancellor of the Exchequer); the Development Act (1909) anticipating Keynesian deficit financing; Winston Churchill's labour exchanges (1909); and Lloyd George's National Insurance Act (1911) giving compulsory insurance to certain workers for benefits in times of sickness and unemployment, paid for by the state, the employer, and the employee – these and a host of smaller measures constituted the first legislative milestones of the modern welfare state. They were based on the rejection of the Victorian principle that individual probity and diligence would ensure modest prosperity: the reforms accepted that capitalism was wasteful, inefficient, and punishing to individuals regardless of personal merit, and that 'voluntaryism' was not enough. But they were nonetheless the reforms of free traders who believed that marginal adjustments to the system could phase out the injustices of capitalism and make it 'fair'.

Taxation and the Lords

These reforms were expensive but based on a wide measure of consensus; it was the raising of revenue to pay for them which caused particular controversy, a controversy compounded by the need to raise large sums to pay for a fleet of *Dreadnought* battleships to match German naval expansion. The Tariff Reformers advocated protective indirect taxes to raise such revenues: the Liberals legislated for expanded direct taxes. Lloyd George's budget of 1909 brought a long-festering issue to a head by introducing a 'super-tax' on the incomes of the very rich and an attempt at an effective tax on land. Balfour and the Unionists used the House of Lords to throw out the budget.

This was the culmination of increasing use of the Lords to frustrate Liberal legislation: the Home Rule Bill of 1893 and a series of measures in 1906–8 had been either mutilated or destroyed. The rejection of the budget, traditionally the prerogative of the Commons, struck at a central tenet of British representative government. The Unionists argued that the conventional exemption of financial legislation meant that Liberals were using it to 'tack' on what was really social legislation – but all taxation was, and always had been, ultimately social in its consequences. Two general elections in 1910 left the Liberals dependent on Labour and Irish support, but nonetheless with a clear majority against the Lords: the Unionist leadership – though not all its followers – eventually conceded the point and the Parliament Act of 1911 limited the Lords' veto to two years.

Home Rule

This great institutional battle had begun with a basic question about social organization: where would the extra tax burden fall – on the rich through the super-tax or on the poor through food taxes? Its progress raised another, about constitutional organization. For the Liberals, as required by their Irish supporters, now introduced the third Home Rule Bill, which, together with disestablishment of the Anglican Church in Wales, became law under the provisions of the Parliament Act in 1914, though suspended in practice for the duration of the war.

The Unionists reluctantly swallowed the budget, but Home Rule they would not stomach. With implicit encouragement from their new leader, Andrew Bonar Law (who replaced Balfour in 1911), they took literally the slogan coined by Lord Randolph Churchill in 1886: 'Ulster will fight and Ulster will be right.' Guns, many of them German, were shipped to Northern Ireland. There was doubt about the loyalty of the army to the State. Three times denied possession of power by the electorate of the United Kingdom as a whole, the Unionists brought Ireland to the edge of civil war in 1914 despite substantial Liberal concessions on the Ulster question, which might have been introduced rather earlier. The outbreak of the First World War prevented posterity from knowing whether the Unionists would have gone over that edge.

Edwardian Britain was thus a turbulent time for politics and politicians. The resurgence of Liberalism and the Liberals' willingness to come to terms with many problems long delayed or frustrated was a painful business for the Unionists, who continued to regard themselves, in or out of power, as the natural rulers of the nation.

Women

But if an old elite's decline caused the greatest trouble, new, rising forces were also very active. The movement for women's suffrage went back to J. S. Mill's attempt to amend the 1867 Reform Bill to give women the vote. Some progress was made, for some women gained the vote for local elections, and for the synod of the Church of England, and could stand as candidates for local councils, school boards, and the poor law board. But the marginal public role given to middle-class women in the 1870s and 1880s – helping the priest, the doctor, or the MP; being secretary to the charity whose chair was almost always a man; taking university examinations but not degrees – was no longer enough. Exclusion from voting for elections of the imperial Parliament exemplified what had come to be seen as deprivation; the campaign for women's votes was a campaign for a new concept of citizenship.

Millicent Fawcett's National Union of Women's Suffrage Societies, uniting in 1897 a number of well-established organizations, was a broadly based movement of impeccably liberal credentials which made considerable headway. It was, however, outflanked and outshone by the Pankhursts' Women's Social and Political Union (1903). The WSPU increasingly advocated violence against both property and individual politicians, as well as inflicting, through imprisonment and hunger strikes, considerable hardship and even occasionally death upon its members. Whether the WSPU helped or hindered the cause is hard to say: on the one hand, it dramatized it, on the other, its support for violence alienated many potential supporters among MPs and in particular Asquith, the prime minister, and made its legislative success less likely. Despite committed support within the Liberal and Labour Parties, and from a few Unionists, no legislation had been passed by 1914.

Trade Unionism and Labour

The Edwardian years also saw a very considerable expansion of the trade union movement, from 2 million members in 1901 to 4.1 million in 1913. In the years after 1908, price inflation and stationary wages encouraged this burgeoning movement to exert its strength; and there was a series of major strikes in 1910–12, culminating in the first general railway strike in 1911, which Lloyd George, as chancellor, defused – also something of a precedent. Since Labour Party membership could only be held through being a trade union member, and since most trade unions came to be affiliated to the Labour Party (the affiliation in 1909 of the coalminers, the chief union still hitherto supporting the Liberals, was a particular triumph), the Labour Party grew considerably in strength. A wide network of constituency parties was established with a ferment of ideological discussion, much of it necessarily utopian in character (and inspired by William Morris), for the means of implementation was as yet very limited.

The party had a secure base in the Commons, but of a limited size, and considerably dependent on its pact with the Liberals which brought it 29 seats at the 1906 election. Its limited success at elections was not surprising, given that in the sort of industrial seat in which it would expect to succeed, about 60 per cent of adult men were not enfranchised. As yet, the party in the Commons saw itself largely as a pressure group for trade union interests, successfully amending the original Liberal bill so as to prevent the legal incorporation of the unions through the 1906 Trade Disputes Act, the consequence of the Taff Vale case. The Labour Party also intervened on social questions and on foreign policy. This slow progress at Westminster led some trade unionists (notably some of the Welsh miners) to turn to syndicalism, that is, 'direct action' by trade unions to promote workers' control, circumventing MPs, Parliament, and the mechanisms of representative government.

The Labour Party's existence and success, closely linked to the expansion and difficulties of trade unionism, reflected a social, as much as an intellectual, difference from the Liberals. The solidarity of the Labour movement was based on cultural and social affinities, the shared experiences of working people in work and leisure, as much as any articulated perception of themselves as a separate class. Working people did not feel themselves to be alienated from the propertied classes, but they did feel themselves to be different. The Liberals reinforced this by their failure to adopt working men as candidates: however broad the agreement on policy matters, the middle-class members of the Liberal Associations – the people who called the tune in the constituencies – would not adopt as candidates men whom they would expect to enter their houses by the servants' door.

Chapter 24

'Your English Summer's Done'

The refurbished Liberalism of the Edwardian years thus faced many difficulties. Legislatively, it met these dynamically and imaginatively with the first of the two great reforming governments of the century. It successfully contained and in large measure resolved the crisis over fiscal policy, welfare policy, socialism, and militarism which had brought many Continental nations to a political impasse by 1914 (though Ireland remained potentially an exception to this). It was not domestic divisions which were to bring Liberal governments in Britain to an end, but foreign affairs.

Anglo-German Hostility

We noted earlier the ambivalent consequences of the entente policy pursued by Lord Lansdowne, Balfour's foreign secretary, and between 1905 and 1914 by Sir Edward Grey for the Liberals. Britain was committed implicitly and emotionally, but not in terms spelt out, to the French–Russian side of the European equation. Secret military conversations after 1905 between the British and the French increased this commitment. Although the greatest imperial power, Britain could bring little direct influence to bear on Continental affairs. R. B. Haldane's army reforms developed an Expeditionary Force intended for Europe, but, though efficient, it was tiny compared to the vast, conscript armies of the Continental powers. Indeed, the Germans simply discounted it, to their cost.

As the concept of the 'Concert of Europe' gave way to overtly nationalistic self-assertion, the British contribution waned. Though personally strongly anti-German, Grey continued to avoid formal alliances, but by 1910 it was clear that Germany would be Britain's adversary, if it were to have one. In a series of incidents in North Africa, the Balkans, and Turkey, and in the continuing escalation of the navy building programme (despite British attempts, especially in 1911–12, to negotiate a limitation agreement), Anglo-German hostility became confirmed. It began to take on a cultural as well as a diplomatic and military aspect. The respect mixed with concern characteristic of British views of German achievements in the 1890s began to change to alarm and fear.

The Onset of War

When events in the Balkans and Central Europe in June and July 1914 led rapidly to war, as Germany estimated that the moment for her bid for mastery had come, the British could bring little influence to bear. Britain had less to gain from war than any of the other major European powers except perhaps Russia. Whether the Liberal Cabinet would have entered the war at all had the Germans not invaded Belgium is open to doubt. But the Germans ignored both the traditional British concern for the strategic importance of the Low Countries, and the implications of guarantee of Belgian independence which they as well as the British had signed in 1870 to last during the Franco-Prussian War. The attack on Belgium decided the matter, and Asquith led his Cabinet into war with only two resignations – John Morley and John Burns. He did so with a heavy heart: the blithe spirit which infused the enthusiastic rush to the colours to join the war that was to be 'over by Christmas' was not shared by Britain's political leadership.

Britain was remarkably unprepared psychologically and, on the whole, physically for a Continental land war. War on land, even in the Crimea and South Africa, had been seen as a marginal matter, to be fought by professionals and a few volunteers. Military values were influential amongst the aristocracy and gentry and increasingly in the public schools, but elsewhere made little impact. Attempts by groups to militarize society – from the Militia of the 1800s through the Rifle Volunteers of 1859 to Lord Roberts's National Service League in the 1900s – had conspicuously failed. 'Trafalgar Day' was the annual martial celebration, reflecting the essentially naval and defensive cast of the public mind – the 'blue water' policy, as it was called. Except in certain rural areas, 'to go for a sodger', 'to take the King's shilling', had for ordinary people been an act of desperation in a time of unemployment or personal catastrophe.

The British public liked bands and bright uniforms because they were entertainments, the exact opposite of harbingers of war. Pomp and domesticity was the British style. Government contracts for guns and ships were by the Edwardian years considerable in value and an important part of the economy of the north east of England, but, in general, military matters seldom impinged on the thinking of government and society. Certainly, they had not penetrated the very fabric of the political, social, and economic order as they had in virtually every Continental state. The first industrial nation had offered the world a remarkable public experiment in liberal, capitalist democracy whose success was premised upon free trade and world peace. Tuesday 4 August 1914 brought that experiment to an abrupt halt.

> There's a whisper down the field where the year has shot her yield,
> And the ricks stand grey to the sun,
> Singing:– 'Over then, come over, for the bee has quit the clover,
> And your English summer's done.'
>
> Rudyard Kipling, 'The Long Trail'

Further Reading

General

G. Best, *Mid-Victorian Britain* 1851–1870 (London, 1971), a predominantly
    social account.

A. Briggs, *The Age of Improvement* (London, 1959), a good political and
    social survey of the period up to 1867.

C. Cook and B. Keith, *British Historical Facts, 1830–1900* (London, 1975),
    includes economic as well as election and ministerial data.

R. C. K. Ensor, *England, 1870–1914* (Oxford, 1936, often reprinted), still
    has material and analysis of value.

E. Halévy, *England in 1815* (Paris, 1913, London, 1924), an early but still
    authoritative account.

E. Halévy, *History of the English People in the Nineteenth Century*, vols 5
    (*Imperialism and the Rise of Labour*, 1895–1905) and 6 (*The Rule of
    Democracy*, 1905–1914) (rev. edn London, 1951–2), a classic account,
    based on contemporary published material, which still holds its own.

J. F. C. Harrison, *Early Victorian England, 1835–1850* (London, 1973),
    particularly strong on protest and radical movements.

G. S. Kitson Clark, *The Making of Victorian England* (London, 1962), like
    G. M. Young a high Tory, but unusually sensitive to the nature of
    middle-class reforming movements.

D. Read, *England 1868–1914* (London, 1979), a competent, detailed
    survey.

G. M. Young, *Victorian England: The Portrait of an Age* (Oxford, 1936), a key reappraisal, rescuing the nineteenth century from the likes of Lytton Strachey.

J. S. Watson, *The Reign of George III, 1760–1815* (Oxford, 1960).

E. L. Woodward, *The Age of Reform, 1815–70* (Oxford, 1960).

Economic

F. Crouzet, *The Victorian Economy* (London, 1982), a synthesis of recent research by the leading French authority on the British economy.

C. Hadfield, *British Canals* (London, 1950), an introduction to his great series of regional histories.

E. Hobsbawm, *Industry and Empire* (London, 1968), an incisive argument, stressing the socio-economic shift from industry to commerce.

D. Landes, *The Unbound Prometheus. Technological Change, 1750 to the Present* (Cambridge, 1969), the relationship of technology to industry.

P. Mantoux, *The Industrial Revolution of the Eighteenth Century* (1911, London, 1961), pioneer and, despite its age, still perceptive study by a French historian.

P. Mathias, *The First Industrial Nation* (2nd rev. edn London, 1983), a clear and concise account.

R. J. Morris and J. Langton (eds), *Atlas of Industrializing Britain* (London, 1986).

M. Robbins, *The Railway Age* (London, 1962), thematic study of railways and society.

L. T. C. Rolt, *Victorian Engineering* (Harmondsworth, 1970), stress on mechanical engineering.

Society and Culture

The Batsford series, *Victorian and Edwardian Life* in photographs (many vols by city and county) is excellent; an important source.

Lady F. Bell, *At the Works* (London, 1911 edn), vivid and acute analysis of social life in Middlesbrough.

A. Briggs, *Victorian Cities* (London, 1963), and *Victorian People* (2nd edn London, 1965), stimulating essays.

O. Chadwick, *The Victorian Church*, 2 vols (3rd edn London, 1971), a powerful survey, rather favourable to Anglicanism.

H. J. Dyos and M. Wolff (eds), *The Victorian City*, 2 vols (London, 1973), splendidly comprehensive illustrations.

C. Emsley, *British Society and the French Wars, 1793–1815* (London, 1979), draws on much untapped archive material.

J. Foster, *The Class Struggle in the Industrial Revolution* (London, 1974), well-researched Marxist interpretation of industry and politics in South Shields, Northampton, and Oldham.

V. A. C. Gatrell, B. Lenman, and G. Parker, *Crime and the Law: The Social History of Crime in Western Europe since 1500* (London, 1980).

J. F. C. Harrison, *Robert Owen and the Owenites* (London, 1969).

F. D. Klingender, *Art and the Industrial Revolution* (London, 1972), Marxist interpretation of art and industry, from optimism to doubt, c.1750–1850.

G. Mingay (ed.), *The Victorian Countryside*, 2 vols (London, 1981), the complementary work to Dyos and Wolff.

H. Perkin, *The Origins of Modern English Society, 1780–1881* (London, 1969).

R. Porter, *English Society in the 18th Century* (Harmondsworth, 1982).

D. Read, *The English Provinces* (London, 1964), social background to industrial revolution and Anti-Corn Law League.

R. Roberts, *The Classic Slum* (London, 1971), childhood in Salford.

B. Simon, *Studies in the History of Education, 1790–1870* (London, 1960), strong on nonconformity and educational innovation.

L. Stone, *The Family, Sex and Marriage, 1500–1800* (London, 1977), changes in family organization, mores, and emotions.

L. and J. C. F. Stone, *An Open Elite? England 1540–1880* (Oxford, 1984).

E. P. Thompson, *The Making of the English Working Class* (London, 1963), a controversial masterpiece.

E. P. Thompson, *Whigs and Hunters* (London, 1975), law and society in the eighteenth century.

F. Thompson, *Lark Rise to Candleford* (Oxford, 1945, often reprinted), the Oxfordshire countryside in decline.

W. R. Ward, *Religious Society in England, 1790–1950* (London, 1972), deals with the complex beliefs and geographies of religion, particularly dissent.

R. Williams, *Culture and Society, 1780–1950* (London, 1958), study of the social critical condition: Burke, Cobbett, Carlyle, Ruskin.

Politics and Government

R. Blake, *Disraeli* (London, 1966), the standard life.

R. Blake, *The Conservative Party from Peel to Thatcher* (new edn London, 1982), the party's fall and rise.

A. Briggs (ed.), *William Morris. Selected Writings and Designs* (London, 1962), gives a useful introduction to the arts and crafts movement.

A. Briggs (ed.), *Chartist Studies* (London, 1974), emphasizes geographical diversity of movement.

M. Brock, *The Great Reform Bill* (London, 1973), the 1832 Reform Act.

H. A. Clegg, A. Fox, and A. F. Thompson, *A History of British Trade Unions Since 1889*, vol. i, *1889–1910* (Oxford, 1964), indispensable account of the complexities of politics and industrial relations.

A. V. Dicey, *The Relation between Law and Public Opinion in England in the Nineteenth Century* (London, 1906), lucid, influential but simplistic approach.

S. E. Finer, *Edwin Chadwick* (London, 1952), study of the great Benthamite reformer.

J. Harris, *Unemployment and Politics. A Study in English Social Policy 1886–1914* (Oxford, 1972; paperback 1984), a powerful critique of the early years of the welfare state.

E. J. Hobsbawm and G. Rue, *Captain Swing* (London, 1968), the labourers' revolts of 1831.

N. McCord, *The Anti-Corn-Law League* (London, 1975).

O. MacDonagh, *A Pattern of Government Growth* (London, 1961), a study of passenger ship regulation as an example of administrative development.

R. McKibbin, *The Evolution of the Labour Party, 1910–1924* (Oxford, 1974, paperback 1983), the standard work on the party's early years.

H. C. G. Matthew, *Gladstone, 1809–1874* (Oxford, 1986).

K. O. Morgan, *The Age of Lloyd George* (3rd edn London, 1978), the best introduction to Liberalism after Gladstone.

H. Pelling, *Popular Politics and Society in Late Victorian Britain* (London, 1968), a volume of challenging reinterpretations.

M. Pugh, *The Making of Modern British Politics 1867–1939* (London, 1982), an intelligent synthesis of recent research.

J. Ridley, *Palmerston* (London, 1970).

A. Rosen, *Rise Up Women!* (London, 1974), places the suffragette movement in a searching light, with unflattering consequences.

P. Smith, *Disraelian Conservatism and Social Reform* (London, 1967), sets Conservative social policy in context.

D. Thompson, *The Chartists* (Aldershot, 1986).

J. Vincent, *The Formation of the Liberal Party, 1857–1868* (London, 1966), a brilliant if sometimes excessively paradoxical analysis.

B. and S. Webb, *The History of Local English Government* (London, 1908–29).

Scotland, Ireland, and Wales

E. D. Evans, *A History of Wales, 1600–1815* (Cardiff, 1976).

C. Harvie, *Scotland and Nationalism* (London, 1977), lively and original.

F. S. L. Lyons, *Ireland since the Famine* (London, 1971), authoritative, from an Anglo-Irish viewpoint.

K. O. Morgan, *Rebirth of a Nation: Wales 1880–1980* (Oxford and Cardiff, 1981), a sympathetic account from a moderately nationalist perspective.

G. O'Tuathaigh, *Ireland before the Famine, 1798–1848* (Dublin, 1972).

T. C. Smout, *A History of the Scottish People* (London, 1969).

T. C. Smout, *A Century of the Scottish People, 1830–1950* (London, 1986).

Imperialism

D. K. Fieldhouse, *The Colonial Empires* (London, 1966), an excellent survey.

P. Kennedy, *The Realities behind Diplomacy* (London, 1981), offers a useful survey of the relationship of diplomacy to power.

R. Robinson and J. Gallagher, *Africa and the Victorians* (London, 1961), a bold thesis, arguing the superiority of strategic over economic motivation.

A. J. P. Taylor, *The Struggle for Mastery in Europe, 1848–1918* (Oxford, 1954, often reprinted), a powerful analysis of the consequences of Germany's bid for power.

A. J. P. Taylor, *The Troublemakers* (London, 1956, reprinted 1969), a heartfelt account of a tradition which failed.

A. P. Thornton, *The Imperial Idea and its Enemies* (London, 1959), an elegant and witty account of the imperial debate.

Chronology

1809–10	Commercial boom
1811	Depression because of Orders in Council; 'Luddite' disturbances in Nottinghamshire and Yorkshire; George, Prince of Wales, made Prince Regent
1813	East India Company's monopoly abolished
1815	Battle of Waterloo: defeat of Napoleon; peace in Europe: Congress of Vienna; Corn Law passed setting price of corn at 80s. per quarter
1815–17	Commercial boom
1817	Slump; the Blanketeers' march and other disturbances
1819	Peterloo massacre: troops intervene at mass reform meeting, killing 11 and wounding 400
1820	Death of George III; accession of George IV
1821–3	Famine in Ireland
1824	Commercial boom
1825	Trade unions legalized; Stockton and Darlington railway opens; commercial depression
1829	Catholic emancipation, ending most denials or restrictions of Catholic civil rights, ownership of property, and holding of public office
1830	Death of George IV; accession of William IV; Liverpool and Manchester railway opens
1830–2	First major cholera epidemic; Whigs in power under Earl Grey
1831	'Swing' riots in rural areas against the mechanization of agriculture
1832	Great Reform Bill brings climax to period of political reform, enlarging the franchise and restructuring representation in Parliament
1833	Factory Act limits child labour; beginning of Oxford Movement in Anglican Church; slavery abolished in the British Empire
1834	Poor Law Amendment Act starts union workhouses; Robert Owen founds the Grand National Consolidated Trades

	Union: action by government against 'illegal oaths' in unionism results in failure of GNCTU and transportation of six 'Tolpuddle Martyrs'
1835	Municipal Reform Act extends local government franchise to all ratepayers
1835–6	Commercial boom: 'little' railway mania
1837	Death of William IV; accession of Queen Victoria
1838	Anti-Corn Law League established; People's Charter drafted
1839	Chartist riots
1840	Penny post instituted
1841	Tories in power: Peel ministry
1843	Church of Scotland splits; Hong Kong leased
1844	Bank Charter Act; Rochdale Co-operative Society founded; Royal Commission on Health of Towns
1844–5	Railway mania: massive speculation and investment leads to building of 5,000 miles of track; Potato Famine begins in Ireland
1845	Famine in Ireland
1846	Famine in Ireland; Corn Law abolished; Whigs in power
1847	Report on Welsh education
1848	Famine in Ireland; Young Ireland rising; revolutions in Europe; cholera epidemic; Public Health Act
1851	Great Exhibition; Catholic hierarchy in England restored
1852	Earl of Derby's first minority Conservative government
1852–5	Earl of Aberdeen's coalition government; reform of Oxford and Cambridge
1853	William Gladstone's first budget
1854	Northcote–Trevelyan civil service report
1854–6	Crimean War, defending European interests in the Middle East against Russia
1855	Viscount Palmerston's first government
1857–8	Second Opium War opens China to European trade; Indian Mutiny

1858–9	Derby's second minority Conservative government
1858	India Act
1859	Publication of Charles Darwin's *Origin of Species*
1859–65	Palmerston's second Liberal government
1860	Anglo-French 'Cobden' treaty and Gladstone's budget codify and extend principles of free trade
1861	Death of Albert, Prince Consort
1862	Limited Liability Act provides vital stimulus to accumulation of capital in shares
1865	Death of Palmerston (October)
1865–6	Earl Russell's second Liberal government
1866	Cholera epidemic; Russell–Gladstone moderate Reform Bill fails
1866–8	Derby's third minority Conservative government
1867	Derby–Disraeli Reform Act; Dominion of Canada Act
1868	Benjamin Disraeli succeeds Derby as prime minister (February); Trades Union Congress formed
1868–74	Gladstone's first Liberal government
1869	Suez Canal opened; Irish Church disestablished
1870	Irish Land Act; Forster–Ripon English Elementary Education Act; Married Women's Property Act extends the rights of women in marriage
1871	Abolition of University Tests
1872	Scottish Education Act
1873	Gladstone government resigns after defeat on Irish Universities Bill; Disraeli declines to take office; economic slump in Europe
1874–80	Disraeli's second Conservative government
1875	Disraeli buys Suez Canal shares, gaining a controlling interest for Britain; agricultural depression deepens; Trades Disputes Act legalizes picketing
1875–6	R. A. Cross's Conservative social reforms passed
1876	Victoria proclaimed empress of India; massacres of

	Christians in Turkish Bulgaria provoke anti-Turkish campaign in Britain, led by Gladstone
1877	Confederation of British and Boer states in South Africa
1878	Congress of Berlin; Disraeli announces 'peace with honour'
1879	Trade depression; Zulu War: British defeated at Isandhlwana, win at Ulundi
1879–80	Gladstone's Midlothian Campaign denounces imperialism in Afghanistan and South Africa
1880–5	Gladstone's second Liberal government
1880–1	First Anglo-Boer War
1881	Irish Land and Coercion Acts
1882	Britain occupies Egypt; Triple Alliance between Germany, Austria, and Italy
1884–5	Reform and Redistribution Acts
1885	Death of Charles Gordon at Khartoum; Burma annexed; Salisbury's first (minority) Conservative government; partition of Africa at conference of Berlin; Scottish Land Act
1886	Royal Niger Company chartered; gold found in Transvaal; Gladstone's third Liberal government introduces first Home Rule Bill for Ireland: Liberal Party splits
1886–92	Salisbury's second (Conservative–Liberal–Unionist) government
1887	British East Africa Company chartered
1888	County Councils Act establishes representative county authorities; Scottish Labour Party founded
1889	London dock strike; British South Africa Company chartered
1890–1	Parnell splits Irish National Party
1892–4	Gladstone's fourth (minority) Liberal government
1893	Second Home Rule Bill rejected by the Lords; Independent Labour Party founded
1894–5	Earl of Rosebery's minority Liberal government
1895–1902	Marquess of Salisbury's third Unionist ministry
1896–8	Sudan conquered

1898	German naval expansion begins
1898–1902	Second Anglo-Boer War
1899	(Autumn) British disasters in South Africa
1900	'Khaki election' won by Salisbury; formation of Labour Representation Committee; Commonwealth of Australia Act
1901	Death of Victoria; accession of Edward VII
1902	Arthur Balfour's Education Act; Anglo-Japanese alliance
1902–5	Balfour's Unionist government
1903	Joseph Chamberlain's Tariff Reform campaign starts
1904	Anglo-French *entente*
1905–8	Campbell-Bannerman's Liberal government
1906	Liberals win general election (January); Labour Party formed; HMS *Dreadnought* commissioned
1907	Anglo-Russian *entente*
1908–15	Herbert Asquith's Liberal government
1908	Asquith's Old Age Pensions plan introduced
1909	Winston Churchill's Employment Exchanges introduced; David Lloyd George's budget rejected by Lords; Union of South Africa Act
1910	(January) General election: Liberal government retains office
	(May) Death of Edward VII; accession of George V
	(December) General election: Liberal government again retains office
1911	Parliament Act curtails power of the House of Lords, establishes five-yearly elections; Lloyd George's National Insurance Act; Moroccan crisis
1911–12	Railway, mining, and coal strikes
1912	Anglo-German navy talks fail; *Titanic* sinks
1912–14	Third Home Rule Act (for Ireland) and Welsh Church Disestablishment Act passed, but suspended
1914	(28 June) Assassination of Archduke Ferdinand at Sarajevo
	(4 August) British Empire enters the First World War

Prime Ministers 1789–1914

(William Pitt	*Dec. 1783)*
Henry Addington	Mar. 1801
William Pitt	May 1804
William Wyndham Grenville	Feb. 1806
Duke of Portland	Mar. 1807
Spencer Perceval	Oct. 1809
Earl of Liverpool	June 1812
George Canning	Apr. 1827
Viscount Goderich	Aug. 1827
Duke of Wellington	Jan. 1828
Earl Grey	Nov. 1830
Viscount Melbourne	July 1834
Duke of Wellington	Nov. 1834
Sir Robert Peel	Dec. 1834
Viscount Melbourne	Apr. 1835
Sir Robert Peel	Aug. 1841
Lord John Russell	June 1846
Earl of Derby	Feb. 1852
Earl of Aberdeen	Dec. 1852
Viscount Palmerston	Feb. 1855
Earl of Derby	Feb. 1858
Viscount Palmerston	June 1859
Earl Russell	Oct. 1865

Earl of Derby	June 1866
Benjamin Disraeli	Feb. 1868
William Ewart Gladstone	Dec. 1868
Benjamin Disraeli	Feb. 1874
William Ewart Gladstone	Apr. 1880
Marquess of Salisbury	June 1885
William Ewart Gladstone	Feb. 1886
Marquess of Salisbury	July 1886
William Ewart Gladstone	Aug. 1892
Earl of Rosebery	Mar. 1894
Marquess of Salisbury	June 1895
Arthur James Balfour	July 1902
Sir Henry Campbell-Bannerman	Dec. 1905
Herbert Henry Asquith	Apr. 1908

Index

Expand your collection of
VERY SHORT INTRODUCTIONS

Visit the
VERY SHORT
INTRODUCTIONS
Web site

www.oup.co.uk/vsi

➤ **Information** about all published titles

➤ News of **forthcoming books**

➤ **Extracts** from the books, including titles
not yet published

➤ **Reviews** and views

➤ **Links** to other **web sites** and main
OUP web page

➤ Information about **VSIs in translation**

➤ **Contact** the editors

➤ **Order** other **VSIs** on-line

VERY SHORT INTRODUCTIONS

Derived from the best-selling *Oxford Illustrated History of Britain*, the following British history titles are now available in the Very Short Introductions series:

➤ **Roman Britain**
Peter Salway

➤ **The Anglo-Saxon Age**
John Blair

➤ **Medieval Britain**
John Gillingham & Ralph A. Griffiths

➤ **The Tudors**
John Guy

➤ **Stuart Britain**
John Morrill

➤ **Eighteenth-Century Britain**
Paul Langford

➤ **Nineteenth-Century Britain**
Christopher Harvie & H. C. G. Matthew

➤ **Twentieth-Century Britain**
Kenneth Morgan

POLITICS
A Very Short Introduction
Kenneth Minogue

In this provocative but balanced essay, Kenneth Minogue discusses the development of politics from the ancient world to the twentieth century. He prompts us to consider why political systems evolve, how politics offers both power and order in our society, whether democracy is always a good thing, and what future politics may have in the twenty-first century.

'This is a fascinating book which sketches, in a very short space, one view of the nature of politics … the reader is challenged, provoked and stimulated by Minogue's trenchant views.'

Ian Davies, *Talking Politics*

'a dazzling but unpretentious display of great scholarship and humane reflection'

Neil O'Sullivan, University of Hull

www.oup.co.uk/vsi/politics

LITERARY THEORY
A Very Short Introduction
Jonathan Culler

Literary Theory is a controversial subject. Said to
have transformed the study of culture and society in
the past two decades, it is accused of undermining
respect for tradition and truth, encouraging suspicion
about the political and psychological implications of cultural products instead of admiration for great literature.
In this Very Short Introduction, Jonathan Culler explains
'theory', not by describing warring 'schools' but by
sketching key 'moves' that theory has encouraged and
speaking directly about the implications of cultural theory
for thinking about literature, about the power of language,
and about human identity. This lucid introduction will be
useful for anyone who has wondered what all the fuss is
about or who wants to think about literature today.

> 'It is impossible to imagine a clearer treatment of the sub-
> ject, or one that is, within the given limits of length, more
> comprehensive. Culler has always been remarkable for
> his expository skills, and here he has found exactly the
> right method and tone for his purposes.'
>
> **Frank Kermode**

www.oup.co.uk/vsi/literarytheory